2-27-67

SHALL WE OVERCOME?

SHALL
WE
OVERCOME?

*A Challenge to Negro and
White Christians*

Howard O. Jones

FLEMING H. REVELL COMPANY

WESTWOOD, NEW JERSEY

The Scripture quotations in this publication are all from the *King James Version of the Bible.*

Portions from a speech made by Martin Luther King, Jr., in Washington, D.C., 1963, appear on pp. 18–19. Copyright © 1963 by Martin Luther King, Jr. Reprinted by permission of Joan Daves.

Material on pp. 22–23, quoted from a column by Roy Wilkins, in the July 24, 1965, issue of the *New York Amsterdam News,* is reprinted by permission of the *New York Amsterdam News.*

Selections by Robert Hall Glover on pp. 84 and 86–87 are from the book *Progress of World-Wide Missions,* reprinted by permission of the publisher, Harper & Row, Publishers, Inc.

The words to the anthem "Lift Every Voice and Sing," by James Weldon Johnson (pp. 145–146), are reprinted by permission of the publisher, Edward B. Marks Music Corp.

*Dedicated to
my wife, Wanda, whose
Christian witness and manner
of life led me to the Saviour.*

Introduction by Billy Graham

For ten years Howard Jones has been associated with me in the work of evangelism. I have had opportunity to observe his life and work very closely. He is one of the most dedicated and committed Christians I have ever known.

He has been used of God to proclaim the Gospel on every Continent, and wherever he has gone we have received glowing reports of his ministry. He is a personal friend of many of the political and religious leaders of Africa. No one in America knows Africa better or loves Africa more. His daily radio program across Africa is listened to by tens of thousands of Africans.

His ministry in America is growing, until now he is in demand from coast to coast to address conferences, to be interviewed on television, to write articles, lecture at colleges, and hold evangelistic crusades.

Howard Jones has helped broaden and deepen my understanding of the religious aspect involved in the civil-rights struggle in America. In *Shall We Overcome?* we sense something of the passion and burden of his heart. He preaches the Gospel as clearly and straight as any man—but he also implements it to the deepest social needs of the nation.

We pray that this book will be used to awaken, arouse, humble, challenge, and convict people of all races who may read it.

BILLY GRAHAM

Preface

For years the spiritual condition of the Negro people has disturbed me, and in the present Negro revolution in America I am more deeply concerned. Admittedly, Negroes are better off materially and financially than ever before. Their annual twenty billion dollars or more of economic power is reflected in fashionable homes, cars, clothes, bank accounts, and the pursuit of many pleasures.

On the other hand, it is quite obvious that spiritual progress is not commensurate with increasing economic prosperity and accumulation of material possessions. As time passes, the Negro becomes more indifferent and often antagonistic to the spiritual verities of life. Deeply engrossed with the world, its problems and pleasures, he appears unconcerned about his eternal destiny. Forsaking the God of his forefathers, he worships the gods of materialism, pleasure, prestige, and power. Blinded by his insatiable desire for worldly possessions, he fails to realize that material prosperity without Christ may prove a curse, for "Man shall not live by bread alone, but by every word that proceedeth out of the mouth of God" (MATTHEW 4:4).

With what result? An avalanche of sin, crime, vice, violence, and lawlessness. The Negro has drifted far from God and broken His commandments, and God is displeased with his waywardness.

Within the Negro church and Christian ministry there is a spiritual apathy and deadness. Many churches are desecrated by courtship and compromise with the world. Recently I read in a Negro newspaper that a group of jazz musicians visited a few churches and a seminary, conducting what they called a "jazz church service." One concert was named: "In the Beginning God. . . ." The newspaper reported that the musicians played ". . . many traditional hymns with a strong rhythmic beat, using selections from the Scriptures and arranging the music and Biblical passages in form of a service. . . ."

Externally the church today has the necessary machinery for work, but lacks the dynamic power of God to effectively represent her Lord and carry out His redemptive program in this turbulent world. The spiritual condition of many churches today is an exact duplication of that of the church of Laodicea in the first century. Christ analyzed the spiritual life of that church, declaring: "I know thy works, that thou art neither cold nor hot: I would thou wert cold or hot. So then because thou art lukewarm, and neither cold nor hot, I will spew thee out of my mouth. Because thou sayest, I am rich, and increased with goods, and have need of nothing; and knowest not that thou are wretched, and miserable, and poor, and blind, and naked: I counsel thee to buy of me gold tried in the fire, that thou mayest be rich; and white raiment, that thou mayest be clothed, and that the shame of thy nakedness do not appear; and anoint thine eyes with eyesalve, that thou mayest see. As many as I love, I rebuke and chasten: be zealous therefore, and repent. Behold, I stand at door, and knock: if any man hear my voice, and open the door, I will come in to him, and will sup with him, and he with me. To him that overcometh will I grant to sit with me in my throne, even as I also overcame, and am set down with my Father in his throne. He that hath an ear, let him hear what the Spirit saith unto the churches" (REVELATION 3:15–22).

In addition to the current civil-rights movement, we need an invasion by the Spirit of God, a moral and spiritual catharsis and renewal, beginning in the church and extending throughout the length and breadth of the race. In this crisis hour, the

8

Negro people require spiritual help and direction. A spiritual vacuum exists that only Christ and the church can fill. It is imperative that the Negro people repent of their sins and turn to Jesus Christ, who alone is the world's hope. If they remain in spiritual bankruptcy, God will frustrate all plans for future progress and humble them before their enemies as He did the children of Israel. The full price eventually to be exacted for moral and spiritual deterioration is an outpouring of God's wrath and judgment.

Admittedly, white churches also need revival. Many have lost their love and devotion for Jesus Christ and His Word, and wander in the wilderness of liberalism, worldliness, and apostasy. On the other hand, we observe evangelical churches that testify of the love of God, preach the whole Bible, and ". . . earnestly contend for the faith which was once delivered unto the saints" (JUDE 1:3), but cling to their old racist and bigoted attitudes toward Negroes.

Not everyone will agree with what I say here. Some will accept the message, others reject it. Truth makes friends and also enemies. However, knowing that God inspired me to "write the vision," I am trusting Him for the results. As "a voice crying in the wilderness," I pray that through the reading of this book sin-weary and spiritually hungry souls may find salvation, peace, freedom, reality, and the hope of eternal life in Jesus Christ. If so, my efforts in writing will be rewarded.

I am indeed grateful for the help and counsel I received from many friends as I prepared this manuscript. A special word of appreciation is given to: Dr. David J. Fant, Dr. Sherwood Wirt, Rev. Louis Johnson, Rev. Elliot J. Mason, Dr. M. C. Southerland, and Rev. Edward H. Holmes.

I also want to thank Bea Maxfield and her secretarial staff for a competent job in typing the manuscript.

I wish to give special thanks to my faithful wife, who read the manuscript and graciously offered inspiration, encouragement, and help during the months of research, study, and writing.

The book is sent forth with the prayer that God will bless its message to many people, causing them to see that with Jesus Christ *we shall overcome.*

For whasoever is born of God overcometh the world: and this is the victory that overcometh the world, even our faith. Who is he that overcometh the world, but he that believeth that Jesus is the Son of God? (I JOHN 5:4, 5).

Howard O. Jones

ST. ALBANS, NEW YORK

Contents

SHALL WE OVERCOME?

*And the Lord answered me, and said, Write
the vision, and make it plain upon tables, that he
may run that readeth it. For the vision is yet for
an appointed time, but at the end it shall speak,
and not lie: though it tarry, wait for it; because it
will surely come, it will not tarry.*

(HABAKKUK 2:2, 3)

1

The Negro in American Society

ONE HUNDRED YEARS ago Abraham Lincoln signed the Emancipation Proclamation. Since that time the Negro's emergence from slavery, his slow but steady progress in spite of many seemingly insurmountable obstacles, has been one of the most remarkable accomplishments of any race in history.

Such phenomenal progress of the Negro in America has not been without sacrifice. Brought to this country against his will, the Negro was subjected to all sorts of hardships and sufferings in his bitter life of servitude. In his book *The Fire Next Time,* James Baldwin takes a long look into the Negro's past; "This past, the Negro's past, of rope, fire, torture, castration, infanticide, rape, death and humiliation; fear by day and night, fear as deep as the marrow of the bone; doubt that he was worthy of life, since everyone around him denied it; sorrow for his women, for his kinfolk, for his children, who needed his protection, and whom he could not protect; rage, hatred, and murder, hatred for white men so deep that it often turned against him and his own, and made all love, all trust, all joy impossible—this past, this endless struggle to achieve and reveal and conform a human identity. . . ."

It was from such a dark, dismal past that the Negro stepped forth. Strangely, the sorrows, sufferings, and hardships of slavery did not defeat or destroy him. Slavery was cruel, unjust, evil, and shameful, but it challenged and inspired the Negro to overcome his many handicaps and make his contribution to the development and welfare of America.

An *Ebony* magazine editorial, entitled "What the Negroes Have Done for America," makes this comment: "It is often said that the American Negro has come further, faster than any other racial group. It might also be added that he has had more obstacles to overcome. His phenomenal progress alone makes him more of a political asset to his country than a burden to the budgets of its public agencies. And despite the admitted handicaps the Negro faces, his list of accomplishments are long and enviable.

"A Negro astronomer made the first American clock and laid out the streets of Washington, D.C. A Negro botanist did more than any single man to advance the science of chemurgy in the utilization of Georgia pine for paper pulp (extracting wealth from the soil). From the soya bean a Negro chemist developed cortisone for the treatment of arthritis, sex hormones for the treatment of expectant mothers, and a fire smothering base for a foam used by the Navy to save thousands of lives. A Negro doctor organized the first blood bank, another performed the first successful operation on the heart, a third man was the first to use aureomycin on human beings."

The record of such achievements by Negro Americans increases with time. Immediately there comes to mind such well-known names as Frederick Douglas, Booker T. Washington, George Washington Carver, Martin Luther King, Ralph Bunche, Thurgood Marshall, Carl Rowan, Roy Wilkins, Marian Anderson, and Jackie Robinson. These products of American soil establish beyond all doubt that when given an equal chance the Negro can prove his worth in every phase of American life.

He would be blind indeed who believes that the Negro is satisfied with his accomplishments. Justly proud of every advancement, he is yet restless and discontent. Within his heart is the gnawing realization that he is a long way from full equality of status in America. He is still confronted with obstacles which threaten to discourage him in his gallant fight for first-class citizenship. Only too well is he conscious of the fact that the color of his skin is a mark against him in white America. The great Negro poet, Paul Laurence Dunbar, expressed it this way:

> We smile, but, O great Christ, our cries
> To thee from tortured souls arise.
> We sing, but O the clay is vile
> Beneath our feet, and long the mile;
> But let the world dream otherwise,
> We wear the mask!

A gifted American leader of the struggle for justice writes: "The Negro is a sort of seventh son, born with a veil, and gifted with the second-sight in this American world, a world which yields him no true self-consciousness, but only lets him see himself through the revelation of the other world. It is a peculiar sensation, this double consciousness, this sense of always looking at one's self through the eyes of others, of measuring one's soul by the tape of a world that looks on in amused contempt and pity. One ever feels his twoness—an American, a Negro, two souls, two thoughts, two unreconciled strivings; two warring ideals in one dark body, whose dogged strength alone keeps it from being torn asunder."

In Ralph Ellison's *Invisible Man* we read: "I am an invisible man. No, I am not a spook like those who haunted Edgar Allan Poe; nor am I one of your Hollywood-movie ectoplasms. I am a man of substance, of flesh and bone, fibre and liquids—and I might even be said to possess a mind. I am invisible, understand, simply because people refuse to see me. Like the bodiless heads you see sometimes in circus sideshows, it is as though I have been surrounded by mirrors of hard distorting glass. When they approach me they see only my surroundings, themselves, or figments of their imagination—indeed, everything and anything except me."

And James Weldon Johnson observed: "This is the dwarfing, warping, distorting influence which operates upon each and every colored man in the United States. He is forced to take his outlook on all things, not from the viewpoint of a citizen, or a man, or even a human being, but from the viewpoint of a colored man. It is wonderful to me that the race has progressed as broadly as it has, since most of its thought and all of its activity must run through the narrow neck of this one funnel."

The late President, John F. Kennedy, was fully aware of the Negro's plight in America. In his message to Congress on February 28, 1963, he said: "The Negro baby born in America today—regardless of the section or state in which he is born—has about one half as much chance of completing high school as a white baby born the same place on the same day—one third as much chance of completing college—one third as much chance of becoming a professional man—twice as much chance of becoming unemployed—about one seventh as much chance of earning ten thousand dollars per year—a life expectancy which is seven years less—and the prospects of earning only half as much.

"No American who believes in the basic truth that all men are created equal, that they are endowed by their Creator with certain unalienable rights, can fully excuse, explain, or defend the picture these statistics portray. Race discrimination hampers our economic growth by preventing the maximum development and utilization of our manpower. It hampers our world leadership by contradicting at home the message we preach abroad. It mars the atmosphere of a united and classless society in which this nation rose to greatness. It increases the costs of public welfare, crime, delinquency, and disorder. Above all, it is wrong."

In a radio and television address to the nation on June 11, 1963, President Kennedy remarked: "The heart of the question is whether all Americans are to be afforded equal rights and equal opportunities, whether we are going to treat our fellow Americans as we want to be treated. If an American, because his skin is dark, cannot eat lunch in a restaurant open to the public, if he cannot send his children to the best public school available, if he cannot vote for the public officials who represent him, if, in short, he cannot enjoy the full and free life which all of us want, then who among us would be content to have the color of his skin changed and stand in his place? Who among us would then be content with the counsels of patience and delay?"

When he succeeded to office, President Lyndon B. Johnson, in an historic address to a joint session of Congress on March 15, 1965, said: ". . . The real hero of this struggle is the American Negro. His actions and protests—his courage to risk safety and even life—have awakened the conscience of the nation. His demonstrations have been designed to call attention to injustice, to provoke change and stir reform. He has called upon us to make good the promise of America.

"And who among us can say he would have made the same progress were it not for his persistent bravery, and his faith in American democracy?

"For at the heart of the battle for equality is a belief in the democratic process. Equality depends not on the force of arms but the force of moral right—not on recourse to violence but on respect for law.

"There have been many pressures upon your President and there will be others as the days come and go. But I pledge you . . . that we intend to fight this battle where it should be fought—in the courts, and in the Congress, and in the hearts of men. . . ."

By comparing the past with the present, it is evident that great progress has been made in race relations in our country. Passage of the Civil Rights and Voting Rights Bills has injected new hope into all Negro Americans. Many schools, hotels, restaurants, and other public places are now totally integrated. However, the Negro is still not completely free from the chains of injustice, nor from social and economic oppression. In some sections of America there are pockets of bitter resistance to the entire civil-rights movement, and to federal legislation which was passed to secure and protect the rights of Negro Americans. Consequently, the long-drawn-out fight for first-class citizenship continues.

The current turmoil reveals the Negro's impatience with all forms of racial segregation and discrimination aimed at him. From the prevalent boycotts and demonstrations we clearly see that a bold spirit of militancy motivates the Negro in his fight for freedom. No longer is he afraid. Willingly he allows himself to be arrested and thrown in jail. The bombing and burning of his homes and churches do no deter him. If need be, he is willing to die for the cause of freedom. Death, indeed, has come to many. Four Sunday-school pupils lost their lives in a church bombing in Birmingham. Medgar Evers was shot to death in Mississippi, and later in that state three CORE workers were murdered. As evidence of injustice, the murderers in these cases have not at the time of this writing been convicted or punished for their crimes.

The current revolt reveals that Negroes have been drawn closer together by their common bond of suffering. This was illustrated in the 1963 march on Washington, D.C., and in the Selma march to Montgomery, Alabama, in 1965, with participants from many states.

In those significant and united efforts, the Negro people were calling upon all right-thinking Americans to awake and do something *now* to solve her disgraceful racial problem, and purge herself from insincerity and hypocrisy. At that history-making meeting in Washington, Dr. Martin Luther King and and others reminded America of her responsibility and debt to the Negro people. Dr. King said: "Five score years ago, a great American, in whose symbolic shadow we stand, signed the Emancipation Proclamation. This momentous decree came as a great beacon light of hope to millions of Negro slaves, who had been seared in the flames of withering injustice. It came as a joyous daybreak to end the long night of captivity.

"But one hundred years later, we must face the tragic fact that the Negro is still not free. One hundred years later, the

18

life of the Negro is still sadly crippled by the manacles of segregation and the chains of discrimination. One hundred years later the Negro lives on a lonely island of poverty in the midst of a vast ocean of material prosperity. One hundred years later, the Negro is still languishing in the corners of American society and finds himself an exile in his own land. So we have come here today to dramatize an appalling condition.

"In a sense we have come to our nation's Capitol to cash a check. When the architects of our republic wrote the magnificent words of the Constitution and the Declaration of Independence, they were signing a promissory note to which every American was to fall heir. This note was a promise that all men would be guaranteed the inalienable rights of life, liberty, and the pursuit of happiness.

"It is obvious today that America has defaulted on this promissory note insofar as her citizens of color are concerned. Instead of honoring this sacred obligation, America has given the Negro people a bad check; a check which has come back marked 'insufficient funds'. . . ."

Admitting the forcefulness of Dr. King's argument, and his ability to portray the racial problem as it exists in America, I believe that there is something more to be said.

It is my personal, sincere conviction that the greatest need of the Negro today is neither freedom from the blight of segregation and discrimination nor the securing of civil rights. For beyond the social, political, and economical needs of the Negro people there is another paramount one—spiritual need. As a people, we need to witness a moral and spiritual awakening, for we have drifted far from God and from the spiritual realities to be found only in Him.

Our impoverished spiritual condition is largely ignored by many Negro leaders in their crusade. We struggle to free ourselves completely from the hangover of slavery, but remain blind to the fact that a heavier yoke binds us—the yoke of sin and wickedness. We fight courageously for our freedom and liberties in this world, but remain ignorant of that freedom and liberty from sin which is ours in Christ, the Saviour. We feverishly seek the pleasures and material things of earth, but fail to answer the question of Jesus: "For what shall it profit a man, if he shall gain the whole world, and lose his own soul?" (MARK 8:36). We labor unceasingly to achieve first-class citizenship in this life, but make no preparation for that blessed citizenship reserved in heaven for all true believers.

Several years ago Dr. Benjamin J. Mays, in an article entitled "Have We Forgotten God?" spoke as a prophet. In part, he said: "I am a bit disturbed about the religious life of the Negro in the United States. In his noteworthy desire to become integrated into the totality of American life is in danger of forsaking and even belittling the religious faith of his fathers. In the secularism of the modern world he may forget God. Two things may happen to the Negro which I fear have happened to America. The more learned, scientific-minded and cultured he becomes the less religious he may be and the less faith he may have in God and the moral order which undergirds the universe. The second danger lies in the area of progress. It often happens that the more prosperous a people becomes the less reliance there is on God.

"I believe there is more religious indifference on the part of Negroes than ever before. There isn't much outright antagonism to religion but the indifference to it in many areas is terrific. Many people think they can be as religious without ever going to church as they can be by going. And yet they do nothing at home to nourish the spiritual life. They read no great books on religion. They are wholly illiterate when it comes to religion and the Bible. They maintain no private devotional life.

"Only a few able Negro students are going into the ministry. It is conceivable that within the next twenty-five years Negroes may be the most irreligious people in the United States."

As a minister of Jesus Christ, I also view the spiritual plight of the Negro with grave misgivings. I am deeply concerned about these things: spiritual poverty in our churches; the fact that in many jails and prisons Negro inmates are the majority; the increasing number of unhappy marriages, divorces, and broken homes among us; an illegitimacy rate among Negroes of about twenty percent; the enormous sums of money wasted on liquor, gambling, dope, and vice; Negro crime and juvenile delinquency on the increase; Negro murderers, rapists, drunkards, dope addicts, and other criminals who stalk the streets. An apt comparison may be made of the sad spiritual condition of the Negro race today with that of the ancient Jews. Viewing the wickedness of the people of his day, the prophet Hosea said: "Hear the word of the Lord, ye children of Israel: for the Lord hath a controversy with the inhabitants of the land, because *there is* no truth, nor mercy, nor knowledge of God in the land. By swearing, and lying, and killing, and stealing, and committing adultery, they break out, and blood toucheth blood. Therefore shall the land mourn, and every one that dwelleth therein shall languish . . ." (HOSEA 4:1-3).

Too long as a race have we excused ourselves from the moral and spiritual duties and responsibilities in life. Beyond the civil-rights crusade, it is extremely important that we rediscover and practice the moral principles of truth and righteousness that will make us proper citizens in the American way of life. Political freedom and civil rights must be inseparably coupled with moral and spiritual obligations. Louis E. Lomax says: "If the American Negro is going to realize his full role in the American experiment he must become a much more responsible fellow than he is now."

Whitney Young, Executive Director of the Urban League, adds to this thought: "Why . . . should we sit back and let reactionary magazines and newspapers expose the sad truth about the Negro crime rate and other social breakdowns? Why let them expose it and then place their interpretation of what has happened to our people? I say we should tell the truth about our own community. We know about the crime rate—

why lie about it? We know about family breakdown—why say it ain't so? We know about relief stealing—why say the white man is making the figures lie? Let's research and expose these things ouselves. That puts us in the driver's seat; we can say, here is what happened, here is why it happened, let's all pull together to do something about it."

Dr. Martin Luther King has called on his followers "to admit that our standards do often fall short" and to do something about it. "Even the most poverty-stricken among us," he has written, "even the most uneducated among us can have high morals. By improving our standards, here and now we will go a long way toward breaking down the arguments of the segregationist."

When in 1965 a white police officer killed a Negro in Brooklyn, the Bedford-Stuyvesant section was tense and on the verge of a racial war. In a newspaper article, Roy Wilkins called upon both Negro and whites to keep calm, saying: ". . . Even kindergarten logic dictates that everyone, black and white, official and just plain citizen, has an obligation to keep calm. We learned last summer in Harlem that street rallies and protests and marches held in such an emotional-charged atmosphere can trigger a riotous upheaval. . . . Despite what others may say, we Negroes know that there is a police brutality problem. That is not to say that every encounter between Negroes and the police is marked by brutality, nor that every policeman is a manhandler or a killer. It is to say that brutality has happened so often over the years and in all sorts of cities and situations that it is a fact of life. But just as we urge acceptance of what we know to be an unpleasant fact, we must accept the truth that in many cases brutality is not present and that in some instances the police are clashing with bad black characters just as they clash—and properly so—with bad white characters. It is a disturbing development to students of social movements that some persons and groups seem to be bent upon turning the Negro community automatically and unilaterally against the police in any kind of situation. If this should be successful, law and order and protection for the vast body of peaceful Negro citizens would go down the drain. The punks, the hoodlums, the loudmouths, the filthy-tongued and those now operating outside the law would take over. We would have no society in the sense of its being a social organization. We would have anarchy. We desperately need not anarchy, but community discipline, the kind based upon something more substantial than wholesale blame of the people ouside the neighborhoods. We need not only strength enough to protest the wrongs done us, but enough more to condemn wrongs and wrongdoers within the race. . . ."

The Negro of our society cannot justly blame all his sins, sufferings, and sorrows on the white man. Admittedly, during the past 300 years white racists in America have brought misery, suffering, bloodshed, and death to the Negro people. God knows all about this shameful record, and those guilty will be judged for their sins against God and our people.

On the other hand, the Negro is equally responsible before God for his life in this world. In Adam, the common head of the human race, he was created in the image of Almighty God. As such, he is a free, moral being with the will and ability to do right or wrong. Since this is true, do we think that we can sin and live wicked and immoral lives, yet expect God to excuse us? Can we be so foolish as to believe that we can willfully and consistently break the moral laws and commandments of God and not be punished? In the sight of God, how can we justify our conduct in the riots in Harlem, Paterson, Philadelphia, Los Angeles, and other cities, when we disgraced ourselves and hurt the cause of the civil-rights movement by destroying property, by violence, rebellion, looting, and stealing? As Negroes we may be an oppressed people, and victims of many injustices, but does this give us the license to return evil for evil? Does it permit us to sin and ignore our responsibilities to God and society? When it comes to this matter of sin and wrong-doing, God will compromise with no one. His immutable law of retribution arrests and punishes all transgressors, regardless of race, color, or nationality. Does not His Word say: "Be not deceived; God is not mocked: for whatsoever a man soweth, that shall he also reap" (GALATIANS 6:7)?

The history of the Negro in America reveals that God protected, comforted, and sustained him in his long, wearisome journey through the wilderness of bondage and servitude.

Without such divine aid and protection, the Negro slaves could not have survived the cruel sufferings and bitter hardships forced upon them by their masters.

In those tragic days Negroes did not have the NAACP, the Urban League, the Southern Christian Leadership Conference, CORE, and other civil-rights organizations to fight their cause. But they did have God. Their hope was in His love and mercy. They knew deep down in their hearts that He was a God of justice, who honored their faith, courage, and patience and would one day bring deliverance. The Christian testimonies of those slaves and God's miraculous dealings with them are expressed in biographies and in traditional Negro spirituals.

That same protection and spiritual direction are needed in these crisis days. Far too many of our generation feel that they can get along without Jesus Christ and the Bible. In an age of secularism, to a large extent we have become a race of humanists, and no longer trust in the God of our fathers, but, rather, glory in our education, wisdom, talents, accomplishments, earthly possessions, and native strength. Such an attitude is displeasing to Him, who says: ". . . let not the wise man glory in his wisdom, neither let the mighty man glory in his might, let not the rich man glory in his riches: But let him that glorieth glory in this, that he understandeth and knoweth me, that I am the Lord which exercise lovingkindness, judgment, and righteousness, in the earth: for in these things I delight, saith the Lord" (JEREMIAH 9:23,24).

Negro Americans today stand at the crossroads of decision and destiny.

Our sins are grievous in the eyes of God. We sin daily in conversation and conduct. We stand ashamed and guilty before the bar of divine justice, because we have broken God's laws and commandments, as clearly defined in the Bible. Not only are our sins an offense to God, but they are a curse and a hindrance in our struggle for proper recognition by our fellows. Moral deterioration from within has destroyed other races, and the cancer of sin is slowly destroying us. Have we forgotten that "Righteousness exalteth a nation: but sin is a reproach to any people" (PROVERBS 14:34)?

Unless we truly repent of our sins, and experience a true moral rearmament, judgment is sure to fall. God judged the people of Sodom and Gomorrah, and those of many nations for their sin, immorality, pride, and lawlessness. How can we expect to escape His wrath if we fail to humble ourselves before Him and turn from our sins? Does not His Word proclaim that "The wicked shall be turned into hell, and all the nations that forget God" (PSALM 9:17)?

Ours is an hour of both obligation and opportunity. Negro Americans must turn to Jesus Christ, the Saviour. Christ loves us. And the Heavenly Father ". . . is no respecter of persons: But in every nation he that feareth him, and worketh righteousness, is accepted with him" (ACTS 10:34,35).

We must realize that Christ died on the Cross to save us. His precious blood was shed to cleanse us from all our sins. True, Christ was buried in the grave, but He arose for our justification and now lives to give us the power to become true overcomers—those who live dedicated and committed Christian lives for His glory.

Christ can give us the kind of leadership we so desperately need. He can remove our frustrations, dilemmas, disappointments, and discontent, and in their place provide the capacity and strength to love, thereby fulfilling the commandment, "Ye have heard that it hath been said, Thou shalt love thy neighbour, and hate thine enemy. But I say unto you, Love your enemies, bless them that curse you, do good to them that

25

hate you, and pray for them which despitefully use you, and persecute you" (MATTHEW 5:43,44).

As a people, we must realize that Christ can help us solve every problem and furnish the courage and strength to face the future fearlessly. He is the hope of the Negro and of all men in a confused, corrupt, and troubled world.

Let us therefore confess our sins to Christ and show true repentance by forsaking them. Let us by faith receive Him into our hearts. Let us humble ourselves before God and pray, in order that ". . . times of refreshing shall come from the presence of the Lord" (ACTS 3:19). Such a spiritual awakening and renewal will have an impact not only on our own, but also on the rest of the world.

Dr. Benjamin J. Mays has said: "The Negro is in a peculiar position to give religious leadership to America. If he neglects so great opportunity, it will be tragic for the Negro and most unfortunate for America."

2

The Negro Church

RECENTLY, IN TALKING with a Negro businessman in
Harlem, we discussed civil rights and other acute problems of
the Negro in America. Eventually our talk turned to the subject of religion, and I asked: "As you observe the Negro
church today, what is your feeling about it?"

The man thought for a moment and replied: "Preacher, I
believe our Negro church needs to be 'born again,' because the
church is failing to fulfill its moral and spiritual responsibility
to the Negro people."

It was an astute observation. The Negro church has failed,
and is spiritually weak and deficient. Many ministers and
other leaders, representing various denominations, have acknowledged this fact to me on numerous occasions in private
conversations. Even the church members have sensed the lack
of spirituality in their churches and are praying that God will
send a divine visitation and renewal and make the church
what it ought to be.

Increasing numbers of our modern young people are rebel-
ling against the Negro church—the oldest of all Negro institutions. They sincerely believe that their church has failed them,
and left them without hope, totally unprepared to face the
moral and spiritual challenge of this corrupt and perverse
world. No wonder the Negro church is being attacked and
severely criticized. Many people are turning away from the
church because they are sadly disappointed and disillusioned.

These people fail to find adequate instruction and spiritual nourishment and satisfaction for the hunger of their souls.

Why has the Negro church become spiritually impoverished? There are, I believe, two answers to that question: first, the Negro church has lost the vision as to the purpose of the church; secondly, the Negro church has drifted far from the divine pattern and program of the church. Loss of vision and estrangement from God account for the spiritual declension in many of our churches today. It is absolutely necessary, therefore, that the Negro church return to Bible standards. The Bible clearly teaches what the church is to be before God and man.

The church should be a place for divine worship. In the Old Testament we read how the people worshipped God in the tabernacle and in Solomon's temple. Turning to the New Testament, we discover, in the Book of Acts, that the worship service in the early church was centered in and around the Person of Jesus Christ. On this point, James A. Stewart says: "The early believers did not worship or serve an historical Christ. They believed in, and had fellowship with, an exalted Lord. Their lives and words gave a continual witness to this fact. Even the enemy reluctantly took knowledge of their vital witness because they had been in company with Jesus. How amazing! The crucified Redeemer was not only seated at the Father's right hand, but also lived in reality among His people. It was this supernatural presence of the crucified, risen Christ that brought about such conviction of sin among the unsaved. The holy power of the presence of the Head of the church in their midst was that which held them together.

"How sad that often today we gather in the name of the living Christ and yet have no real, revolutionary sense of His presence: How strange it would seem to the average evangelical church if a believer solemnly announced, 'Beloved saints, the living Christ is is our midst this morning; let us welcome and worship Him.' Oh, that He might be more manifestly present in our corporate church life."

28

We need to improve the quality of the worship services in many of the Negro churches. Much of what we call "divine worship" would certainly not have been accepted as such by the early Christians. In most Negro churches today the main emphasis in the worship service is upon anything but Christ himself. We stress ritualism and ceremonialism, and emphasize various kinds of music and singing. In his book *Strength To Love,* Dr. Martin Luther King draws a parallel between two different types of Negro churches and the way they worship. He says: "One burns with emotionalism, and the other freezes with classism. The former, reducing worship to entertainment, places more emphasis on volume than on content and confuses spirituality with muscularity. The danger in such a church is that the members may have more religion in their hands and feet than in their hearts and souls. . . .

"The other type of Negro church . . . has developed a class system and boasts of its dignity, its membership of professional people, and its exclusiveness. In such a church the worship is cold and meaningless, the music dull and uninspiring, and the sermon little more than a homily on current events. If the pastor says too much about Jesus Christ, the members feel that he is robbing the pulpit of dignity. If the choir sings a Negro spiritual, the members claim an affront to their class status. This type of church tragically fails to recognize that worship at its best is a social experience in which people from all levels of life come together to affirm their oneness and unity under God."

It is also true that in most of our churches we take entirely too much time raising money in the worship service. The majority of Negro churches make "money raising" the principal part of the service, sometimes taking several offerings in the same service. All kinds of tricks are used to get more money out of the congregation. Such practices shatter the whole spirit of worship, and lead people to believe that money has become the idol in the Negro church.

Where is Jesus Christ in our worship services? We worship

each Sunday, but there is very little evidence that we have really met Jesus. We meet each other in the church and are mindful of how each of us looks and what clothes we wear, but few of us are conscious of the living Christ in our midst. we may preach about Christ, sing about Him, and even attempt to pray to Him, but our hearts and minds are far from Him. The sad spiritual state of our lives proves this to be true. In the Old Testament, the prophet Micah spoke out against the insincerity of worship among the people of his day, saying: "Wherewith shall I come before the Lord, and bow myself before the high God? shall I come before him with burnt offerings, with calves of a year old? Will the Lord be pleased with thousands of rams, or with ten thousands of rivers of oil? shall I give my firstborn for my transgression, the fruit of my body for the sin of my soul? He hath shewed thee, O man, what is good; and what doth the Lord require of thee, but to do justly, and to love mercy, and to walk humbly with thy God?" (MICAH 6:6–8).

Jesus Himself testified against the people of His day because their worship of God was not right or sincere: "Ye hypocrites, well did Esaias prophesy of you, saying, This people draweth nigh unto me with their lips; but their heart is far from me. But in vain they do worship me, teaching for doctrines the commandments of men" (MATTHEW 15:7–9).

The services in many of our churches must be revamped if we are to have Scriptural divine worship in them. Where ritualism and ceremonialism have hindered and bound us, the service needs to be simplified. In other cases, where there is no real order, the worship service must be planned prayerfully so that everything is done decently and in order. The Bible says that ". . . God is not the author of confusion, but of peace . . ." (I CORINTHIANS 14:33). Beyond that, there is need for spiritual preparation if we are to worship God. Our hearts and lives must be right with God and our fellowmen, or else our worship is in vain. Our Lord says: "But the hour cometh, and now is, when the true worshippers shall worship the Father in spirit and in truth: for the Father seeketh such to worship him. God is a Spirit: and they that worship him must worship him in spirit and in truth" (JOHN 4:23,24).

Too, the church should be a place for Christian fellowship within the redeemed family of God. Its members are truly saved from their sins and born again through a personal encounter with Jesus Christ, the Saviour. The Apostle John speaks of this wonderful Christian fellowship when he says: "That which we have seen and heard declare we unto you, that ye also may have fellowship with us: and truly our fellowship is with the Father, and with his Son Jesus Christ" (I JOHN 1:3).

Apparently, many of our church leaders are unaware of the fact that Christian fellowship in the church is possible only when people measure up to God's standard for membership in the local church. In the Book of Acts, chapter 2, verse 47, we are told what that standard is. Note the last part of the verse: "And the Lord added to the church daily such as should be saved." Here is revealed the one and only true qualification for membership in the church of Jesus Christ—salvation.

In the first-century church only those persons who truly repented and were saved were "added to the church." The addition was not made by the apostles, but by the Lord Himself. No sinner could possibly receive admission into the church, for that church consisted only of born-again believers, those who had been reconciled to God through the death of Jesus Christ, whose names ". . . are written in the Lamb's book of life" (REVELATION 21:27).

In most Negro churches today, there is little or no standard with regard to church membership. The fact is that standards for admission to a country club or a fraternal organization are more rigid than church membership. We are so terribly busy increasing our membership rolls that we allow anyone to join the church, whether spiritually qualified or not. What is the result? We have large churches, but for the most part they are church fellowships of sinners. We can claim only a small minority of genuine, sincere, dedicated Christians. Our churches are overloaded with unconverted members. Many of these people are good church workers and loyal to the church, but they are lost church members because they have never really repented of their sins, nor have they experienced the new birth in Christ Jesus.

We have led our people to believe that the only requirement to become Christians is to come forward when the minister "opens the door" of the church, that if their names are written in the church membership book this will secure for them a place in heaven.

But nowhere in the Bible do we find any justification for such practise. Membership in the fellowship of the church is made possible only through the miracle of the new birth. "The church," Peter Eldersveld says, "is the birthplace of souls. Its members are reborn people. They had to undergo a radical change in order to get in. . . . Making true church members is not like so many other things in the machine age. It is not a gigantic work of mass production. . . . No, the church is a family of individual children born again by the Spirit of God; and at every rebirth there is great rejoicing in heaven."

How wonderful and glorious our churches would be if they could truly become Christian fellowships here on earth. There is no fellowship like that of God's people—one made possible because of vital relationship with Jesus Christ and union with one another. The Bible says: "If we say that we have fellowship with him, and walk in darkness, we lie, and do not the truth: But if we walk in the light, as he is in the light, we have fellowship one with another, and the blood of Jesus Christ his Son cleanseth us from all sin" (I JOHN 1:6,7).

The church is to be a place for prayer. The ministry of prayer was faithfully maintained in the early church. In Acts 3, verse 1, we read: ". . . Peter and John went up together into the temple at the hour of prayer. . . ."

Throughout the Book of Acts we read that the early Christians prayed in times of peace and in time of trouble. Great miracles were wrought by God in the church because those Christians lived in an atmosphere of prayer.

Our Lord also believed in prayer. At times He spent whole nights in prayer. Christ taught that prayer must have its rightful place in the life of the Christian and of the church. One day Jesus visited the temples in Jerusalem. His anger was aroused when He found that the ministry of prayer had been replaced by other business. The record is: "And Jesus went into the temple of God, and cast out all them that sold and bought in the temple, and overthrew the tables of the moneychangers, and the seats of them that sold doves, and said unto them, It is written, My house shall be called the house of prayer; but ye have made it a den of thieves" (MATTHEW 21: 12,13).

The Negro church must return to a real ministry of prayer. We need to meet God in prayer for our own personal lives, and for the crisis we face as a race of people in white America. We have far too many prayerless churches. There may be tremendous crowds on Sunday mornings and on special occasions, such as Christmas, Easter, Mother's Day, or a civil-rights rally. But what about the attendance at the church prayer meeting? The weakest meeting in most of our churches is the prayer service. Some churches have had to discontinue the midweek prayer meeting because the people have ceased to attend.

Prayerlessness in the church and in the life of the Christian is sin in the sight of God. A prayerless church is a powerless church. A prayerless church will not prosper spiritually, nor can it expect to receive the blessings of God upon it. By the ministry of prayer we can judge the spiritual life of any church. We sometimes rate the spirituality of a church by the size of its Sunday morning congregation, but the true church is much more likely to be found in the prayer meeting on Wednesday evening.

If Jesus Christ were to visit many of our churches next

Sunday morning, His anger would again be stirred, and He would drive out the religious racketeers. He would call many of these churches "a den of thieves." Why? Because they, like the temples of old, have replaced the ministry of prayer with worldly programs which should have no place in the Christian church.

Christ wants our churches to be houses of prayer where He may be glorified. How long will it be before we change our churches from social and commercial clubs into real prayer centers? How long will it be before we realize the need of waiting upon God in prayer in our homes and in our churches until God sends a moral and spiritual awakening in our midst? In this crisis hour in the Negro revolution, when uncertainty and trouble surround us and when destruction hovers over the nations, we must pray to God. No longer can we afford to trust the arm of flesh or our own wisdom and intellect; we must pray to the God of heaven, and our hearts must be right with Him and with each other. This is the truth we need to discover in the current civil-rights movement. Too many Negroes try to pray in churches and in public places for the welfare of the race, with malice and an unforgiving spirit in their hearts against others. They try to pray to a God whom they have never known in their own lives. They pray, but they pray using God as a crutch in time of trouble, only to forsake Him when the crisis is over. Such praying will get us nowhere with God. There is power in prayer for those earthly pilgrims whose hearts and lives are right with God.

The church is to reflect the holiness of God. Speaking of the church, the Apostle Peter says: "But ye are a chosen generation, a royal priesthood, an holy nation, a peculiar people; that ye should shew forth the praises of him who hath called you out of darkness into his marvellous light; which in time past were not a people, but are now the people of God: which had not obtained mercy, but now have obtained mercy" (I PETER 2:9,10).

One of the tragedies of our day is that a large percentage of

34

the members in Negro churches do not represent Jesus Christ as they should. They attend church each Sunday; they worship, sing in the choir, take communion, give their money, work in church clubs, and serve in various official capacities in the church. But as far as spirituality and real dedication to Christ are concerned, they are sadly lacking. These people have "a form of godliness," but not the power to live a holy life. As "lovers of pleasures more than lovers of God," they give no real evidence of a born-again experience or of a cleansing of their sins in the precious blood of Christ. They sing, jump up and down, and shout "Amen" and "Hallelujah" in the church on Sunday, and then live "like the devil" the rest of the week by lying, cheating, stealing, getting drunk, gambling, playing the numbers, and committing adultery. This shameful condition brings a reproach upon the name of Christ and makes the Negro church a laughing stock before the eyes of an ungodly world.

While conducting a series of revival meetings in a church in Delaware, the pastor and I visited some of the people in the neighborhood. As we approached one house, the pastor said: "Howard, the man here was once an alcoholic, but he was converted and became an outstanding Christian layman in our church. However, something went wrong in his life, and he slowly drifted from God and returned to his old sinful ways. We have tried many times to get him back to church. I thought I would tell you this before we see him."

We entered the house, greeted the man, and invited him to attend our meetings. He hesitated for a moment and then said: "Preacher, I appreciate this visit from you and the pastor, but I shall not be able to come to your meetings this week."

"Why?" I asked.

"Because I don't believe in playing with God," the man replied. "You see, Preacher, I once knew the Lord. Christ delivered me from a wicked life of drunkenness, and for a time I served God in the church. But after a while I got out of fellowship with the Lord, and soon the old devil led me back to drinking and into sin. So I stopped going to church and I have not been in years."

"Well, now, don't you think it is time for you to get right with God while there is time?" I questioned.

"Preacher," the man continued, "I know that there are plenty of other people in the church who are not living right also. They attend church regularly. They sing and shout, but their lives are bad. In the summer I sit on my porch on Sunday evenings and watch them go to church. Occasionally, I see some of the deacons duck into a nearby alley, and in the semidarkness they take out their bottles and drink, either before or after the service, and then come out into the street as though nothing has happened."

"Now, sir," the man concluded, "if your preaching helps those hypocrites to get right with God, perhaps I too will come back to God and the church. But I don't see why I should sit with those who live just as I do but try to give the impression that they are saints."

We tried to get the man to see that he had a personal responsibility to God, regardless of what others might do or not do, but we failed.

In the midst of the present Negro revolution in America, the Negro church has a tremendous responsibility to set a moral and righteous standard before the world. But it is ignominiously failing to be the "light of the world" and the "salt of the earth." With immorality, sin, and hypocrisy in the church, how can there be respect and honor? As long as the leaven of unrighteousness permeates the church, how can any moral and spiritual influence upon our homes, communities, and the nation be exerted? You cannot raise the moral standard of any community, whether it be black or white, any higher than the standards set by the churches in that community. A corrupt church helps to corrupt a community. But a holy and spiritual church exerts its influence on the community for good. Therefore, the moral and spiritual tone of our

Negro communities in cities across America will be improved to a great extent when our churches reflect more of the righteousness, purity, and holiness of God. However, if church leaders and members continue to live unholy lives, what can be expected of those persons outside the churches? The Bible says that "judgment must begin at the house of the Lord."

God has ordained that the church demonstrate His power. No one can study the Book of Acts without coming to the conclusion that the first-century church had power with God and men. The secret and source of that power was the Holy Spirit. Before Christ ascended into heaven, He informed His disciples that the Holy Spirit would bring spiritual power into their lives which would enable them to conduct an effective ministry of evangelism and missions, beginning at Jerusalem and extending to the ends of the earth. In the Book of Acts, our Lord says: "But ye shall receive power, after that the Holy Ghost is come upon you: and ye shall be witnesses unto me both in Jerusalem, and in all Judaea, and in Samaria, and unto the uttermost part of the earth" (ACTS 1:8).

The glorious fulfillment of Christ's prophecy concerning the Holy Spirit came on the day of Pentecost, the birthday of the Christian church. As the one hundred and twenty disciples waited in the upper room, the Holy Spirit was poured out upon them, their lives were transformed, and the church moved forward in supernatural power to perform great exploits for God.

One could very well ask: "Where is the power of the Holy Spirit in many of the Negro churches today?" Thank God for a few churches here and there where one can sense the real presence and power of the Spirit of God. Sinners find the Saviour, and Christians continue to grow in grace and in the knowledge of Jesus Christ. But the fact remains that the majority of our churches lack the "wind" and the "fire" of the Holy Spirit. The breath of God is sadly missing in them.

In most Negro churches there is an abundance of emotionalism. It is absolutely sickening to the seeker for spiritual reality to observe the way some church members work themselves into a wild emotional frenzy by screaming, shouting, praying, jumping, twisting, jerking, singing, and handclapping—behavior which is more fitting to a circus than a house of God.

We cannot produce the power of the Holy Spirit through human means or efforts. Emotionalism stimulated and controlled by the Holy Spirit may have its place. But emotionalism produced merely by the cunning efforts and tricks of people apart from the influence of the Holy Spirit is nothing but fleshly power. It is utterly devoid of spiritual profit or edification.

In the Negro church we need to rediscover the Person and power of the Holy Spirit. In our church creeds we confess: "I believe in the Holy Ghost." But do we really believe in Him? Are we really conscious of His Presence? We Christians will have to recognize, honor, obey, and be led of the Holy Spirit if we want our lives and churches to be endued with power from on high. God says, "Not by might, nor by power, but by my Spirit."

The power of the Holy Spirit is needed so that the Negro church will exercise the Scriptural rule of discipline. The rule of discipline was used in the Old Testament against persons who sinned. We read how Joshua dealt with Achan because Achan had sinned in the camp of Israel and caused Israel's defeat at Ai. Achan was judged and sentenced to death (JOSHUA 7).

The rule of discipline was also used in the early church. An example is the account of Ananias and Sapphira, who sinned by withholding part of their offering from their church. This couple also lied so as to cover up their sin. They were disciplined. Swift judgment and death fell upon them (ACTS 5:1–11).

The Apostle Paul exercised the rule of discipline in his ministry. A member of the church of Corinth was guilty of immorality. Paul dealt with this person so as to maintain a holy and righteous standard in the church (I CORINTHIANS 5:1–5). Whenever the Holy Spirit is in control of a church, the rule of discipline will operate to keep church members in step with the truth of the Gospel.

But instead of following lofty Scriptural standards, the rule of discipline has almost vanished from modern church life. Every member feels that he can do that which is right in his own eyes. Church leaders and members sin and walk contrary to the Word of God without fear that the church will judge them for their wrong. If anything, we make excuses for people who sin. And the more prominent a church member, the easier it is for that person to do wrong and get away with it. This evil practice explains to a great extent why so much hypocrisy and sinful living exists in our churches. How can we have a healthy spiritual church, one possessed with the power of God, if there is no standard of righteousness, and church members are not disciplined when they do wrong?

This lack of discipline explains why there is so much squabbling and dissension at many of our annual church conventions. In fact, you can hardly believe that you are at a church conference when you see what goes on in the name of God at some of these meetings. Tempers flare, abusive remarks are made, violence erupts, and fights break out, sometimes even among ministers. Occasionally, the police have to be summoned to maintain peace and order. Dr. Nathan Hare, in his provocative article "Have Negro Ministers Failed Their Roles," recalls: "When the Baptist group flocked to Kansas City for the 1961 event, the mayor met them with warm words of welcome, saying in effect, according to *The Chicago Crusade:* "Welcome—but go home if you came here to raise cain."

These "spiritual leaders" (including some well-known advocates of passive resistance and nonviolence) proceeded to do just that. At one point, a coterie of clergymen stormed the pulpit in an effort to keep the claimant to the throne off the speaker's platform. This resulted in the death of an elderly pastor and part-time mortician from Detroit, who fell off the back of the platform with another minister on top of him.

Not all Negro church conventions and conferences follow such a pattern. It is refreshing to visit conventions where there is a spirit of unity and love among the brethren, and where things are done decently and in order.

But even on the local church level we are plagued from time to time with trouble and discord among the church leaders and members. These churches do not have the spiritual power to control adequately the conduct of its constituency. Sometimes a church fight will break out. The trouble usually starts over a moral problem, or a problem of leadership and power, or because some church official has either stolen on misappropriated church funds. The two opposing sides line up against each other, and the battle spreads like a prairie fire throughout the church and into the community. The disgraceful mess is publicized in the newspapers and brought into court for resolution. In some cases the minister is guilty, and the judge will rule that he should leave the church. A padlock is sometimes placed on the church door to prevent the minister from returning to the church.

At other times the judge rules against the body of reactionary members of the church who plot to oust the faithful minister and ruin the church. No wonder there are so many church splits; no wonder unsaved and unchurched people look on the disgraceful behavior of so-called Christians and say: "If that's the church, I will have no part of it."

It is my personal conviction that no church should go to court to solve its problems. There is no perfect church among the visible churches on earth. Every church has its share of problems; the New Testament churches had theirs. However, churches ought to be spiritual enough to solve their problems without taking them into secular courts for solution. The Apostle Paul proclaimed this truth to the church of Corinth: "Dare any of you, having a matter against another, go to law before the unjust, and not before the saints? Do ye not know that the saints shall judge the world? and if the world shall be judged by you, are ye unworthy to judge the smallest matters? Know ye not that we shall judge angels? how much more things that pertain to this life? If then ye have judgments of things pertaining to this life, set them to judge who are least esteemed in the church. I speak to your shame. Is it so, that there is not a wise man among you? no, not one that shall be able to judge between his brethren? But brother goeth to law with brother, and that before the unbelievers. Now therefore there is utterly a fault among you, because ye go to law one with another. Why do ye not rather take wrong? why do ye not rather *suffer yourselves to* be defrauded? Nay, ye do wrong, and defraud, and that *your* brethren" (I CORINTHIANS 6:1-8).

Surely we need to look to the Holy Spirit for the necessary power and courage to establish and maintain discipline in our churches. The Negro church must judge all sin in the light of the Word of God. It must discipline its leaders and members whose lives and conduct are displeasing to Christ and inconsistent with the Gospel.

In this present evil world, the Holy Spirit is needed to give us power to live dynamic and dedicated lives for Jesus Christ. I talked not long ago with a prominent Negro minister who is president of the ministerial conference of his denomination. Our conversation dealt with the spiritual condition of the Negro church today. Among the many things he said was this: "One of the great problems facing us as ministers in the Negro churches today is that we have very few really outstanding, sincere and dedicated Christians in these churches. Most of our members are not dedicated to anything. They do not know what the Christian life is. Consequently, they have no fire or power to live a consistent Christian life. Some of the followers of false cults and religions put our church members to shame when it comes to the matter of dedication to what they believe and the sacrifices they are willing to make to advance their cause. Our church drastically needs a moral and spiritual awakening."

He was right. We have lost the spiritual dynamism in our

churches. Church members are not contributing much to the cause of Christ in terms of consecrated living and service. But once the Negro church experiences a spiritual revolution in its midst and yields itself to the leadership and control of the Holy Spirit, we will witness a new church among us, whose leaders and members are truly converted and on fire for God. In that ideal church you will not have to beg members to attend church, give tithes, support the prayer meetings and Bible classes, and seek to win the unsaved to Christ. Filled with the power of the Holy Spirit, they, like the early Christians, will live holy and dedicated lives for the glory of God. In this crisis hour, God is calling the church to repentance and revival. Will the Negro church answer His call and rise from her sin and spiritual bankruptcy and impotency? It is either now or never. God's promise comes in the form of a challenge when He says: "If my people, which are called by my name, shall humble themselves, and pray, and seek my face, and turn from their wicked ways; then will I hear from heaven, and will forgive their sin, and will heal their land" (II CHRONICLES 7:14).

3

The Negro Ministry

IN THE UNITED STATES, from the early days of slavery until the present, the Negro minister has made a commendable contribution to the welfare and advancement of his race. He is the recognized leader of the masses. His close, intimate contact with the people through the church gives him a preeminent position of leadership, and a power surpassing that of his fellows.

On this subject, the heart-searching book *Souls of Black Folk* says: "The preacher is the most unique personality developed by the Negro on American soil. A leader, a politician, an orator, a 'boss,' an intriguer, an idealist—all these he is . . . the combination of a certain adroitness with deep-seated earnestness, of tact with consummate ability, gave him his preeminence, and helps him maintain it."

Because of its position and potentiality, the impoverished spiritual condition of our Negro ministry is cause for deep concern. Like the church, the ministry is failing to provide the proper moral and spiritual leadership for the people. It desperately needs spiritual renewal. Too long the "men of the cloth" have excoriated the sins and weaknesses of their church members, while at the same time thay have closed their eyes to their own shortcomings. The time has come for the powerful, penetrating searchlight of God's Word—the Bible to be turned on shepherd as well as sheep. Preachers must take a hard look at their own hearts and lives. They must see themselves as God sees them. Such spiritual examination is imperative if the Negro ministry is to regain the dignity, respect, and influence it once had.

The Bible has much to say concerning the Christian ministry. We must turn to it for a formula for faith and a standard for conduct. The Negro minister must know that his life and service are according to the will of Almighty God.

Consider the minister as a man. According to the Bible, he must be a converted man. When speaking to Nicodemus, an outstanding religious leader of his day, Jesus said: ". . . Verily, verily, I say unto thee, Except a man be born again, he cannot see the kingdom of God. . . . That is born of the flesh is flesh; and which is born of the Spirit is spirit. Marvel not that I said unto thee, Ye must be born again" (JOHN 3:3,6,7).

On this point J. K. Bolarin says: "It is imperative that any person who is in a position of leadership in the church must be a 'born-again' Christian. He must be able to give a clear testimony as to his personal experience of salvation from sin through faith in Christ, and he must show clear evidence in his life of a true change of heart."

The biographies of some of the pioneer Negro ministers during the slavery period in America are inspiring and challenging. These men, representing different denominations, confessed to a personal cataclysmic conversion in Jesus Christ —one that brought a revolutionary change in their hearts and lives. Among the Baptists there were such spiritual giants as George Liele and Andrew Bryan—men who became great preachers because of their warm-hearted devotion to Jesus Christ, the Word of God, and the souls of men. Their ministry in the South had a tremendous impact upon both Negro and white.

Bishop Richard Allen, founder of the Africa Methodist Episcopal denomination, was a man of many rare gifts. Like many other Negro ministers of his day, he knew by personal experience the saving grace of God in his own life. Testifying of his conversion, he said: "I went with my head bowed for

44

many days. My sins were a heavy burden. I was tempted to believe that there was no mercy for me. I cried to the Lord both night and day. One night I thought hell would be my portion. I cried unto Him who delighted to hear the prayers of a poor sinner; and, all of a sudden, my dungeon shook. My chains fell off, and 'Glory to God,' I cried. My soul was filled. Enough for me—the Saviour died. Now my confidence was strengthened that the Lord, for Christ's sake, had heard my prayers and pardoned all my sins. I was constrained to go from house to house, exhorting my old campanions, and telling to all around what a dear Saviour I had found."

In our day, Bishop Allen's testimony of a genuine conversion may sound strange and fanatical to many popular and prominent ministers. Some would describe such a spiritual experience as too otherworldly, and not in keeping with our modern, scientific age.

But such an experience is fundamental. One only needs to observe a group of ministers as they meet for their weekly session or during a church conference or convention. Listen carefully to their conversation. There are discussions of practically everything and anything—church problems, current events, civil rights, even that which is frivolous and vulgar. If the matter of a man's need for Christ or his relationship to the Master is mentioned, more often than not a dead silence falls on the assembly. There is only a cold spirit of indifference and unconcern.

Is it not sad that so few of our Negro ministers can give a clear-cut, positive testimony to a born-again experience in Jesus Christ? Surely the spiritual leader should be able to relate what Christ has done in his own life. The Bible says: "But sanctify the Lord God in your hearts: and be ready always to give an answer to every man that asketh you a reason of the hope that is in you with meekness and fear" (I PETER 3:15).

Christ should be no stranger to the minister, nor the minister a stranger to Christ. But far too many of our church pulpits are filled with unregenerate men—sinners in clerical robes who preach about Christ, but in reality know nothing whatsoever of His saving grace and cleansing power. What a tragedy! For how can our churches prosper spiritually when those in charge are void of spiritual power? In God's sight, unconverted ministers are no asset to the churches they lead. Like the scribes and Pharisees of Christ's day, these men are outwardly religious. They pray long prayers and expound their teachings, but they knew not the reality of Christ, the Saviour. Jesus condemned such men of His generation, by saying: "Let them alone: they be blind leaders of the blind. And if the blind lead the blind, both shall fall into the ditch" (MATTHEW 15:14).

We need to pray that the Spirit of God will move upon the hearts of Negro ministers. Like the members of their churches, they must repent of their sins and have a personal experience of Jesus Christ. When there is such an experience, spiritual power and blessing will follow, and the church will share the spiritual renewal.

Unfortunately, many men get into the Christian ministry without first finding Christ as their personal Saviour. But God is merciful, and He gives even unconverted ministers a chance to repent and get right with God. Often in the Billy Graham crusades, ordained ministers come forward to receive Christ as Saviour. What a thrilling testimony these men later give of their new-found faith and the reality of His presence in their lives. These men return to their churches with a burning desire to preach the Christ they now know by personal experience. It is humbling for a minister to confess conversion after serving in the church for years. But far worse would it be to die in sin and lose his soul. The judgment of God will be more severe on those who have had the light but have not walked in it. We Negro ministers must search our hearts. Have we truly been saved from our sins? Have we been born of the Spirit of God? Do we know the reality of the presence of the living Christ in our lives? If not, let us repent and meet the Saviour

46

now. Tomorrow may be too late. It is written in the Bible: ". . . behold, now is the accepted time; behold, now is the day of salvation" (II CORINTHIANS 6:2). "The Lord is not slack concerning his promise, as some men count slackness; but is long-suffering to us-ward, not willing that any should perish, but that all should come to repentance" (II PETER 3:9). How shall we escape, if we neglect so great salvation . . ." (HEBREWS 2:3).

The man who enters the ministry should be called of God. His is the highest calling known among men. What a high privilege and honor it is to be chosen of God to preach the Gospel, the unsearchable riches of Christ, to lost humanity.

In the Bible we often read of the divine summons. In Genesis 12:1-3 is the account of the call of Abraham. Later Moses responded to the call of God to deliver his people from their oppressors. The method is instructive: "Now Moses kept the flock of Jethro his father in law, the priest of Midian: and he led the flock to the backside of the desert, and came to the mountain of God, even to Horeb. And the angel of the Lord appeared unto him in a flame of fire out of the midst of a bush: and he looked, and, behold, the bush burned with fire, and the bush was not consumed. And Moses said, I will now turn aside, and see this great sight, why the bush is not burnt. And when the Lord saw that he turned aside to see, God called unto him out of the midst of the bush, and said, Moses, Moses. And he said, Here am I" (EXODUS 3:1-4).

To the prophet Isaiah came the call of God: "Also I heard the voice of the Lord, saying, Whom shall I send, and who will go for us? Then said I, Here am I; send me. And he said, Go, and tell this people . . ." (ISAIAH 6:8,9).

God also called the prophet Jeremiah: "Before I formed thee in the belly I knew thee; and before thou camest forth out of the womb I sanctified thee, and I ordained thee a prophet unto the nations" (JEREMIAH 1:5).

In the New Testament the Apostle Paul tells of the summons that came to him: "But I certify you, brethren, that the gospel which was preached of me is not after man. For I neither received it of man, neither was I taught it, but by the revelation of Jesus Christ. . . . But when it pleased God, who separated me from my mother's womb, and called me by his grace, to reveal his Son in me, that I might preach him among the heathen; immediately I conferred not with flesh and blood" (GALATIANS 1:11,12,15,16).

In light of the above, must we not in all honesty confess that in large measure we have lost the Biblical concept of the Christian ministry? Many Negroes have come to look upon the ministry with growing disgust and contempt. An illustration of this came to me while talking with an elderly Negro woman in Cleveland, Ohio. Discovering that I was a minister, and the father of four daughters and a son, she opened her heart. "For God's sake, don't bring up that boy of yours to be a preacher," she counseled.

"Why?" I asked.

"Send him to college and let him prepare himself to become a doctor or lawyer, and make something out of himself. Anybody can be a preacher. You don't need to know anything. All you need to do is to get out in the street and holler real loud. You get a crowd, and soon have a church."

It was easy to see that she had a low estimate of the ministry, one from which I was not able to dissuade her.

There are among us varying opinions of what the Christian ministry really is. Some consider it to be a good profession, a respectable white-collar job, with unlimited opportunities for religious, social, and political service, and now especially work for civil rights. There are those who consider the ministry to be a good opportunity to acquire prestige, power, advancement, and material gains. Others "take up the ministry" because of pressure from their minister, parents, or friends. And there are those who turn to the ministry as a last resort after having failed in some other field of employment. There is neither time nor space for all the reasons. But one thing is sure. Our ministry is filled with men who in God's sight should be outside looking in. Why? Because God has never called them to the divine and sacred task. This is a tragic fact, but true.

The serious problem of misfits in the ministry is nothing new. God had a controversy with certain men in Jeremiah's day who were engaged in the ministry, but had never been called by Him to be prophets. They ran about preaching their doctrines and relating their dreams to the people, but God had no part in them. Of them God said: "I have not sent these prophets, yet they ran: I have not spoken to them, yet they prophesied" (JEREMIAH 23:21).

We must recover the truth that the Christian ministry is a unique holy calling of God to man. The initiative is with Him, and we have no right to choose the ministry ourselves. The Sovereign God of heaven has the sole authority to choose. He places man in His service according to His will. The apostle bears his own witness to this fact: "And I thank Christ Jesus our Lord, who hath enabled me, for that he counted me faithful, putting me into the ministry" (I TIMOTHY 1:12).

Only God-called and God-prepared men can qualify for this sacred task. It is, therefore, dangerous for any man to enter the ministry without being called and chosen by God. Every minister must know that "the agonizing grip of the hand of God" has been laid on him as a minister.

Much harm is being done to our churches because many of them harbor as spiritual leaders those who have entered a profession without first having a possession. It is a popular procedure nowadays for our churches to call a man as pastor on the basis of striking appearance, immaculate dress, academic training, gift of oratory, magnetic personality, or administrative ability. The basis should rather be conversion and call. This is not to imply that academic training and other talents and abilities are to be despised. Rather, it is to put things in their proper order. In the selection of a minister, spiritual qualifications must be of primary concern. A man may be ever so highly trained; he may be a silver-tongued orator. But if God has never called him, it would be better for that man to leave the ministry and seek other employment. For so long as he remains, his work, however good in other respects, can never bring spiritual life and blessing to the church.

Too, the minister needs to be a thoroughly consecrated man. He must live a holy life before God and the people, for God commands: ". . . Be ye holy: for I am holy" (I PETER 1:16).

The priests and prophets, God's ministers of the Old Testament dispensation were commanded to live holy, consecrated lives. Consider Aaron, the high priest. Concerning the consecration of Aaron and his sons, we read: "And the Lord spake unto Aaron, saying, Do not drink wine nor strong drink, thou, nor thy sons with thee, when ye go into the tabernacle of the congregation, lest ye die: it shall be a statute for ever throughout your generations: And that ye may put difference between holy and unholy, and between unclean and clean" (LEVITICUS 10:8-10).

In God's sight and in the sight of the people, Aaron and the priests of his day were to distinguish themselves as holy men of God. "They shall be holy unto their God, and not profane the name of their God . . . they shall be holy" (LEVITICUS 21:6).

The Apostle Paul accepted this requirement. Writing to the church at Corinth he said: "Therefore seeing we have this ministry, as we have received mercy, we faint not; But have renounced the hidden things of dishonesty, not walking in craftiness, nor handling the word of God deceitfully; but by manifestion of the truth commending ourselves to every man's conscience in the sight of God" (II CORINTHIANS 4:1,2).

As ministers, we too need to realize our responsibility to ". . . live soberly, righteously, and godly, in this present world" (TITUS 2:12).

We are ordained to be "ambassadors for Christ"—"ministers of the sanctuary" on earth. Above all else, we should strive to live that men might see the beauty of Christ reflected in us. We must let our lights so shine that men may see our good works and glorify our Father in heaven (MATTHEW 5:16).

A conspicious failure in the ministry of our day is the lack of upright, moral, righteous lives. Admittedly, the validity of such a serious indictment might well be questioned. Far too many of our ministers are involved in questionable activities, and are slaves of vicious habits which bring disgrace and shame upon themselves and reproach upon Christ, the church, and the entire ministry. To many the sky is the limit as far as unholy living is concerned. Like the priests of Ezekiel's day, they profane the holy things of God. ". . . they have put no difference between the holy and profane, neither have they shewed difference between the unclean and the clean . . ." (EZEKIEL 22:26).

Often it appears that the more unholy and immoral the ministers, the more popular they are with their people. Observe, then, their manner of life. Some are drunkards, gamblers, adulterers, homosexuals, and hypocrites. There are those who are dishonest, ruthless, and even cruel in their business dealings. In many instances the Negro ministry has so deteriorated that it is almost void of ordinary morality, integrity, and Christian virtues. It is surprising that many people, both inside the church and out have lost their respect and appreciation for these leaders?

Several years ago I preached in a rather large church in Harlem. After the service, the minister thanked me for the message, and said, "Say, Jones, I bet a young preacher like you has a little sweetheart on the side, don't you?"

Needless to say, I was shocked by his question, but finally I said: "Of course not. I have a lovely wife. She loves me, and I love her. My wife is my sweetheart, and I don't need another one."

I then quoted Revelation 21:8 to him: "But the fearful, and unbelieving, abominable, and murderers, and whoremongers, and sorcerers, and idolaters, and all liars, shall have their part in the lake which burneth with fire and brimstone: which is the second death."

"Now, Jones," the minister continued, "I know what the

Bible says, but you know how it is when you want to pay some attention to the ladies."

Again I challenged him with the Word of God. When he saw that I would not agree with his immoral reasoning, he abruptly ended the conversation by saying: "I was only kidding. I don't want you to think I am a bad fellow. I don't cheat on my wife. My only bad habit is smoking."

I left with a sick feeling. My respect for that prominent minister was gone. I thought: Is this the kind of example young ministers must expect from the eldest men in the ministry? Where is the example of righteousness? What hope is there for young ministers if older ones have such corrupt minds and lives?

Once a minister friend of mine and I visited a large church convention in the South. While eating lunch with one of the host pastors of the convention, we found him quite upset and disgusted. "Would you believe me," he said, "that since this convention has begun I have been plagued with some visiting ministers who informed me that they were here for a good time? They wanted to know if I could help find some women for them. I flatly refused their request and told them that I do not believe in this sort of business, nor did I keep company with the kind of people they were looking for."

The situation has not changed. Some ministers continue boldly and unashamedly to take the opportunity in their church conferences and conventions for a rendezvous with illicit sex and other questionable and worldly pleasures. One minister told me that he secluded himself between sessions, remaining in his room so as not to be propositioned by lewd women who attended the conference. How can we justify ourselves for such wickedness in work relating to Christ and His church?

We must realize that God keeps a close watch over our lives. Our sinful acts are never hidden to His all-searching eyes. "The eyes of the Lord are in every place, beholding the evil and the good" (PROVERBS 15:3). "Neither is there any creature that is not manifest in his sight: but all things are naked and opened unto the eyes of him with whom we have to do" (HEBREWS 4:13).

Immorality is nothing new. It appeared among the prophets. This shameful condition brought grief to the heart of God and to the prophet Jeremiah. Every minister, on his knees, should read these challenging words: "Mine heart within me is broken because of the prophets; all my bones shake; I am like a drunken man, and like a man whom wine hath overcome, because of the Lord, and because of the words of his holiness. For the land is full of adulterers: for because of swearing the land mourneth; the pleasant places of the wilderness are dried up, and their course is evil, and their force is not right. For both prophet and priest are profane; yea, in my house have I found their wickedness, saith the Lord. Wherefore their way shall be unto them as slippery ways in the darkness: they shall be driven on, and fall therein: for I will bring evil upon them, even the year of their visitation, saith the Lord. . . . Thus saith the Lord of hosts, Hearken not unto the words of the prophets that prophesy unto you: they make you vain: they speak a vision of their own heart, and not out of the mouth of the Lord" (JEREMIAH 23:9-12,16).

From these verses we clearly see that the judgment of God will eventually fall upon all who violate God's moral laws. And, in the light of today's corruption, insincerity, and hypocrisy among those who pose as spiritual leaders in our church, one fears that soon the judgment and the wrath of God will fall upon us, and that without mercy. God's wrath struck down Moses and Abihu, the wicked priests and sons of Aaron, because they handled holy things without themselves being holy. They offered "strange fire" before the Lord. How shall we Negro ministers escape the hurricane of the divine wrath if we do not repent of our sins and lead righteous lives?

God's patience must be sorely tried in view of the foolishness and wickedness of so many of our preachers. God has been merciful to tolerate our waywardness so long. This condition has filtered through to the church members, who are grieved and disillusioned by the sins of their pastors. There are laymen who are fasting and praying that God will bring a moral and spiritual catharsis to save the Negro ministry from complete ruin.

Holiness of living! This is God's clarion call to all of us. Some have responded. It is wonderful and encouraging to meet ministers of various denominations whose consecrated living, sincerity of heart, dedication of spirit, and fervent love for Jesus Christ have won the respect, honor, and abiding confidence of the people to whom they minister. These are the true servants of God. Their clean lives and unselfish, sacrificial service are a blessing to all. May their numbers be increased!

Too long have some of our preachers tacitly said to their congregations: "Don't do as I do, but do as I say." We must reject such a Satan-inspired philosophy and endeavor by God's help to live daily according to the lofty ethical standards of the Word of God. It is for us to fear the Lord and walk humbly before the people "as becometh saints."

But something more. The time has come when we must take to heart this moral and spiritual declension and do something about it. And that quickly. Churches and ministerial alliances and conferences must work together to rebuke, discipline, and if necessary unfrock and excommunicate those ministers whose unholy living makes them a curse rather than a blessing. This is no time for silence or compromise—swift, direct action is required if the Negro ministry is to experience moral change and be restored to a place of spiritual power, honor, and dignity.

Now as to our message. What is its substance? This is an important, timely question, one that needs a clear-cut, positive answer. Admittedly, there are many ideas and opinions among us. But since the Bible is our final authority on all matters pertaining to the church and the Christian ministry, let us see what it has to say.

The Bible teaches that the cardinal message of the Christian minister is the Gospel. This Gospel is not of man—that is, not the product or result of man's natural wisdom or understanding. Rather, it is centered in Jesus Christ—God's distinct and unique Revelation to man.

A study of the life and ministry of Christ reveals that He began His wonderful work on earth by preaching and teaching the Gospel with all authority and power. In the Book of St. Mark, chapter 1, verses 14 and 15, we read: ". . . Jesus came into Galilee, preaching the gospel of the kingdom of God, And saying, The time is fulfilled, and the kingdom of God is at hand: repent ye, and believe the gospel."

Throughout His entire ministry, Jesus faithfully proclaimed His Gospel to all men. One day He went into the temple, He opened to the prophecy of Isaiah, and read this prediction concerning Himself: "The Spirit of the Lord is upon me, because he hath anointed me to preach the gospel to the poor; he hath sent me to heal the brokenhearted, to preach deliverance to the captives, and recovering of sight to the blind, to set at liberty them that are bruised, To preach the acceptable year of the Lord. And he closed the book, and he gave it again to the minister, and sat down. And the eyes of all them that were in the synagogue were fastened on him" (LUKE 4:18-20).

And significantly, just before His ascension, Christ emphasized the importance of the Gospel to His disciples, challenging them with The Great Commission: ". . . Go ye into all the world, and preach the gospel to every creature. He that believeth and is baptized shall be saved; but he that believeth not shall be damned" (MARK 16:15,16).

The disciples obeyed His order and the Gospel was ". . . preached every where, the Lord working with them, and confirming the word with signs following" (MARK 16:20).

The message now preached by most Negro ministers is not the pure, unadulterated Gospel of Jesus Christ. More and more we are drifting away from the basic and fundamental doctrines of historic Christianity. Many of our ministers no longer accept the Bible as the inspired and infallible Word of

God. They disagree with some of the creeds and confessions of their church. As one writer says: "They quote authority after authority to tell what He says; they quote poet after poet to relate His idea: but they never mention what God said" (*Development of Negro Religion*).

To a great extent the Negro ministry has substituted "other gospels" for the one and only true Gospel of the Son of God. It has become popular to deliver philosophical, political, social, and ethical sermons. These sermons, which are more in the nature of religious essays, for the most part express the thoughts and wisdom of the preacher, rather than the mind and will of God. Most popular of present-day subjects is the gospel of civil rights. Now, it is quite understandable why the Negro minister has felt called upon to help in the struggle for the first-class citizenship of Negroes. He is the leader of the masses. Consequently, in the civil-rights movement he finds that he must become involved in the fight to free his fellows from the yoke of Jim Crowism and discrimination. It is not easy for a Negro minister to view the sufferings of his people without feeling compelled to do something to aid them. The pressure of circumstances has forced him to speak out against the evils of segregation and discrimination. How can he remain silent when his people are smarting under the whip of injustice, and dying at the hands of the white racists? Negro ministers, therefore, lead in the demonstrations. Sold on the justice of their cause, they allow themselves to be thrown into jail. Certainly, all must admire their courage and sacrifice.

However, in this fight for first-class citizenship something unfortunate has happened. By becoming involved in the civil-rights movement, most of our ministers have lost sight of the main message that God has called them to preach. In the struggle, the Negro minister has allowed himself to be sidetracked. And, instead of preaching the Gospel, the whole counsel of God, instead of rightly dividing the Word of Truth, he has adopted a new message, the gospel of civil rights. When one visits the average Negro church on any given Sunday morning, he will find that to a great extent the message from the pulpit is devoted to civil rights, or to the political affairs of the Negro race and nation, and not to the Bread of Eternal Life. Biblical, expository preaching is almost a lost art. This is most unfortunate, because thereby Satan has gained a great victory. Surely it grieves the heart of God. For the gospel of civil rights is not the Gospel God has called us to preach. This is not the supreme message of the Negro church or any other church. The one who preaches the gospel of civil rights may draw the crowds and makes himself popular. And, unless he preaches such a gospel, many will consider him unfaithful to his race. Since the civil-rights gospel is the one most people want to hear, it is one that helps the one who proclaims it become known through the press, radio, and TV.

God is surely distressed over this situation, for the Negro church has become the sounding board for every gospel save the true one of Jesus Christ.

With what result? When the minister forsakes the supreme message of his high calling, his substitute gospel lacks the spiritual power and the authority of God. The message is painfully weak. We may sway audiences with our oratory, and challenge them to fight for their social and political rights in this world, but such a message does not touch their moral and spiritual life, nor does it prepare them for eternity.

The plain fact is that many of our young people are not being reached with the Christian message. Young men in our congregations are not stirred by the words they hear. This partly explains why so few young men hear the call of God to the Christian ministry. A recent report related that in all of our seminaries there are less than 200 Negro young men preparing for the ministry. This is tragic, for unless our churches give birth to young preachers, our churches will eventually die for lack of leadership. May we not rightly conclude that it is because of our neglect to preach the true Gospel that our young men do not feel the grip of its message upon their hearts and lives? They have never felt the compulsion of the man who said, "Woe is me, if I preach not the Gospel."

Our churches are suffering spiritually because of this de-

57

parture. Only the Gospel of Jesus Christ can feed the hunger and quench the thirst of the human soul. The Gospel is the Bread of Life for all men. Yet, in our churches, both small and large, the members are spiritually famished. An increasing number of church members are weary of the endless politics and philosophies they hear every Sunday morning. Lay members long for the pure Word of God: when it is preached in its fullness it is like a cup of cold water to their thirsty souls. It provides comfort and strength to go forth into a wicked world with hope and confidence.

"My people are destroyed for lack of knowledge. . ." says the Word (HOSEA 4:6). This is as true today as when it was originally uttered. Because the preaching of the Word has been neglected, the average church member is deplorably ignorant of what the Bible teaches. In many churches, when I stand to take my text, scarcely a single person in the church can be seen with a Bible in hand. It is a tragedy that in the Negro church today the Bible is not being taught nor its contents expounded by the ministers. The people are given almost everything else but what they have a right to expect. Asking for bread, they are given a stone. This is a sin before God and heaven.

How can we do God's work without His Word. To quote the Bible: "So shall my word be that goeth forth out of my mouth: it shall not return unto me void, but it shall accomplish that which I please, and it shall prosper in the thing whereto I sent it" (ISAIAH 55:11). And Jesus said: "Heaven and earth shall pass away, but my words shall not pass away" (MATTHEW 24:35).

Our political, racial, ethical, and philosophical gospels are marked for time, not eternity. Such gospels will not save us from our sins, nor prepare us to meet God. In the final analysis, these gospels of men are of little spiritual profit to us.

If there was ever a time when we needed to get back to the preaching of the Word, it is now. Some of us may have to humble ourselves before God and cast our little essays into the flames if we want God's blessing. He honors the man who honors His Word. We must be Bible preachers. Yea, we must be prophets, men who can stand in the pulpit on Sunday and say to our congregations: "Thus saith the Lord." We must be able to read the signs of the times and interpret the trends of this space age so as to make the Bible relevant to the sordid facts of life. For ours is a wicked world of sin, corruption, prejudice, hatred, violence, bloodshed, and murder. Who but ourselves will warn sinners to flee from the wrath of God? The times demand courageous preaching against sin and everything contrary to the truth of the Gospel. We must call our people to repentance and faith in Jesus Christ, the Saviour. It is for us to proclaim the mercy, love, and forgiveness of Christ, that God is not willing that any should perish, but that all should come to repentance. Our people must be confronted with our Lord's searching question: "For what shall it profit a man, if he shall gain the whole world, and lose his own soul?" (MARK 8:36). This kind of preaching would revolutionize our churches and give moral and spiritual direction to their wandering, bewildered members. May the Lord raise up men in this crisis hour who will call our people back to God.

Some of us are deeply disturbed by the strange silence on spiritual matters on the part of prominent civil-rights leaders. These men may be rightfully admired for their sincerity, and for their dedication to the full emancipation of the Negro people. At times they have been subjected to intimidation, persecution, and even death for their protests. But for some reason they have failed consistently to state the essentials of the Gospel message; not a word do they utter about the need for repentance and reformation of life.

The historical march on Washington, D.C., provided an example. There, with 250,000 people gathered at the Lincoln Memorial, not a word was said about the faith of our fathers. The same was true after the march at Selma, Alabama. Could not such occasions have been accepted as providential openings, not only to rebuke the nation for racism, but to point to the true solution of our deepest problems, those which are basic to good character and citizenship, that can only be found when the heart is opened to Jesus Christ? Remember, these were not merely political leaders; these were in large measure ministers of the Gospel, those ordained to reveal the riches of the kingdom of heaven. What would Jesus have done on such an occasion? Or Saint Paul? With the kingdoms of this world offered to Him, Jesus avowed, "My kingdom is not of this world."

Jesus said, "Without me ye can do nothing." Do we believe this? If we do, then we ought to call upon Christ to help us in all of our problems, including the racial struggle.

As a minister, I have experienced something of the power of the Gospel in my own life. It was the Gospel of the cross that lifted me from sin and saved me. Its power gripped my heart and subsequently directed my steps.

With the Apostle Paul I can say: "For I am not ashamed of the gospel of Christ: for it is the power of God unto salvation to every one that believeth . . ." (ROMANS 1:16). "For the preaching of the cross is to them that perish foolishness; but unto us which are saved it is the power of God" (I CORINTHIANS 1:18). "For I determined not to know any thing among you, save Jesus Christ, and him crucified" (I CORINTHIANS 2:2).

And with Pascal I can declare: "The Gospel to me is simply irresistible. Being the man that I am, being full of lust, and pride and envy and malice and hatred and false good, and all accumulated and exaggerated misery—to the Gospel of the Grace of God, and the redemption of Christ, and the regeneration and sanctification of the Holy Ghost, that Gospel is to me simply irresistible, and I cannot understand why it is not equally irresistible to every mortal man born of woman."

Our generation sorely needs a revival of Bible and Spirit-filled preaching. If the Negro pioneer preachers were conscious of the need for preaching the Gospel of the crucified and risen Son of God, how much more aware should we be now. These fearless men blazed trails across this country, not with their own message nor a message their people wanted to hear, but with the redemptive, regenerating Word of Almighty God. And God signally blessed those men and their churches. And He will repeat the process if we humble ourselves, wipe the dust from our Bibles, and expound its message from cover to cover. Such ministerial procedure is Scriptural.

Paul instructed his youthful disciple: "Study to shew thyself approved unto God, a workman that needeth not to be ashamed, rightly dividing the word of truth" (II TIMOTHY 2:15). "I charge thee therefore before God, and the Lord Jesus Christ, who shall judge the quick and the dead at his appearing and his kingdom; Preach the word; be instant in season, out of season; reprove, rebuke, exhort with all longsuffering and doctrine. For the time will come when they will not endure sound doctrine; but after their own lusts shall they heap to themselves teachers, having itching ears; And they shall turn away their ears from the truth, and shall be turned unto fables" (II TIMOTHY 4:1-4).

God is calling for Negro ministers to preach His Gospel to the Negro race, to the nation, and to the world. Who will answer the call? How many will cease being the puppets of men and become true prophets of God to this lost generation? Remember, the Gospel of Christ will save both ourselves and those to whom we minister. For as Dr. Hugh Thomson Kerr says: "We are sent not to preach sociology but salvation; not progress but pardon; not social order, but the new birth; not reorganization but a new creation; not democracy but the Gospel; not civilization but Christ. We are ambassadors, not diplomats."

What, then, should be the Negro minister's chief concern today? Under God, the minister has been made the spiritual shepherd over the flock. He should be the physician of the soul, the one most concerned about the spiritual welfare and growth of his members.

The Apostle Paul had this concern for the people to whom he ministered and whom he loved. To those at Thessalonica he revealed his heart: "But we were gentle among you, even as a nurse cherisheth her children: So being affectionately desirous of you, we were willing to have imparted unto you, not the gospel of God only, but also our own souls, because ye were dear unto us" (I THESSALONIANS 2:7,8).

The Master Himself set the example. Who can equal the love and compassion which He showed for the people of His day? Said He: "I am the good shepherd: the good shepherd giveth his life for the sheep. . . . I am the good shepherd, and know my sheep, and am known of mine. . . . And other sheep I have, which are not of this fold: them also I must bring, and they shall hear my voice; and there shall be one fold, and one shepherd" (JOHN 10:11,14,16).

It is cause for rejoicing when we meet those who take their ministry seriously, who consider it a high and sacred calling. How encouraging it is to meet one who lives a godly life and loves the people of his congregation. Watch him as he faithfully cares for the flock. He feeds, nourishes, and strengthens his people in the Word of God. He comforts and consoles them in the hour of trouble and sorrow. He weeps over their sins, weaknesses, and failures, and endeavors to lead them on into the green pastures of blessing, fruitfulness, and victorious living. In all kinds of weather he visits the sick in homes and hospitals. He has a deep concern for his people, and constantly demonstrates it by his devotion to them, standing ready to minister to their needs whenever required. Such a minister is a rare gift from God to the church.

There are far too few such shepherd-pastors among us. It appears that most of our ministers have lost sight of the primary purpose of their vocation. No longer possessing the shepherd-touch and the shepherd-heart, a great gulf exists between the minister and his people. On this subject Dr. Nathan Hare says: "There is, for one thing, the special extent to which the Negro has experienced the sudden transition from the close, intimate familiarity of farm folk to the cold impersonality of metropolitan life and what that has done to the relations between minister and member. . . . Whereas the pastor's life once bloomed side by side with his flock's, both in and out of the church, the cityward trek of the Negro has brought him to the mass church and Sunday preacher, who is seldom if ever seen closeup by the majority of his members. (This does not exclude the occasional, post-sermon handshake administered by him, or one of his assistant pastors, as members mechanically file from the church building.)

"This separation of the minister and follower has made it ever less likely that the ends of the minister will be of one accord. Quite frequently, in fact, the members find themselves pursuing salvation while their pastors pant after power and glory. In general, the shepherd-pastor has been replaced by the administrator-executive who even resents being called 'preacher' and pompously demands the title 'minister.' Thusly bent on officialdom, he is consumed by a passion for presiding as an end in itself."

We see, then, that many of our ministers are not really interested in people for what they are. They are not much concerned about what they can do to help their congregations become better Christians. Instead, they are mindful of what people have, and how much they extract from them for their own selfish interests. Some merely use the church to support themselves as politicians. Others give special attention to those who are members of the affluent society, but sadly neglect the poor saints in the church.

While I was pastor of a church in New York City, a grief-stricken woman came to my parsonage early one morning. I knew her and the members of her family because we lived in the same community, though they were not members of my church. In tears, the woman related: "Oh, Pastor Jones, I have just received word that my husband was crushed to death by an elevator on his job. I have already made the arrangements with the undertaker to go for the body, and now I am coming to see if you could help me plan the funeral and officiate at the service."

"But," I asked, "aren't you a member of another church here? Have you contacted your pastor?"

"Yes," the woman replied. "I tried to get our pastor, but he was out of the city on business I was told, and that if I wanted him to return for the funeral I would have to pay his fare. I then asked the assistant if he would take charge, but he refused, saying that we could not have the funeral at the church because of its crowded schedule."

The woman continued. "To tell the truth, Pastor Jones, as you know, our church is a very large one, and unless you are a prominent member you cannot expect to receive much help or service from it."

It was hard for me to believe that such heartless, unsympathetic treatment could be given a poor widow in her hour of deep tragedy and sorrow. If ever she needed the spiritual help of her pastor and the church it was then. Yet she was deprived of that privilege because she was not influential enough. The funeral was held at an undertaker's chapel, and I took charge of the service.

In our churches we have developed a class of ministers who function as religious playboys rather than true shepherds. These men devote so much time to social and secular activities that they have little left for a vital spiritual ministry. It is a fact, though a shameful one, that few of our ministers do any pastoral visitation. His colleagues would tab him "old-fashioned" if he did. The popular trend is to relegate visitation to an assistant pastor or to a visitation committee. Is it any wonder that ministers have become strangers to their own congregations?

And what about the church member? Often he is nothing more than a "name" and "number" on the church membership list. Many feel lost in the church. Why? Because they have no sense of belonging; and even in the hour of worship they do not find in their pastor a deep concern for them. Congregations suffer because of lack of spiritual care and attention. As a consequence, many members wander from church to church in search of a minister who is truly dedicated to his task—one who is concerned about their needs.

Good endeavors, even the civil-rights movement, may make too many demands upon the preachers' time. First things first, as the Bible declares: "Woe be unto the pastors that destroy and scatter the sheep of my pasture! saith the Lord. Therefore thus saith the Lord God of Israel against the pastors that feed my people; Ye have scattered my flock, and driven them away, and have not visited them: behold, I will visit upon you the evil of your doings, saith the LORD. . . . And I will set up shepherds over them which shall feed them: and they shall fear no more, nor be dismayed, neither shall they be lacking, saith the Lord" (JEREMIAH 23:1,2,4).

In these perilous days, when the Negro church is so spiritually weak and deficient, its ministers must get back to the fundamentals of their calling. God demands that they serve as the Apostle Paul endorsed, "For the perfecting of the saints, for the work of the ministry, for the edifying of the body of Christ: Till we all come in the unity of the faith, and of the knowledge of the Son of God, unto a perfect man, unto the measure of the stature of the fulness of Christ" (EPHESIANS 4:12,13).

God is calling His ministers to be vigilant watchmen in the church, men who cannot remain silent, but will speak out against sin, Satan, and all the subtle and spurious doctrines and philosophies of men. Such a ministry will bring the blessing of God upon the church. And he who gives himself to this type of ministry will find it to be a full-time job, leaving little time for subordinate activities.

The Apostle Paul's example is an inspiring one, directed to the spiritual leaders in the church at Ephesus: "Wherefore I take you to record this day, that I am pure from the blood of all men. For I have not shunned to declare unto you all the counsel of God. Take heed therefore unto yourselves, and to all the flock, over the which the Holy Ghost hath made you overseers, to feed the church of God, which he hath purchased with his own blood" (ACTS 20:26-28).

And the Apostle Peter advised elders to: "Feed the flock of God which is among you, taking the oversight thereof, not by constraint, but willingly; not for filthy lucre, but of a ready mind; neither as being lords over God's heritage, but being ensamples to the flock. And when the chief Shepherd shall appear, ye shall receive a crown of glory that fadeth not away" (I PETER 5:2-4).

The Negro ministry of the present day has a unique opportunity to make a vital spiritual contribution to its own membership, and to the masses of unsaved and unchurched Negroes in the American society. To make such a contribution, however, the Negro clergy must immediately overcome its sins, and shake off its apathy and indifference. The pressures, tensions, and revolutionary changes wrought by the current civil-rights movement in America have created a spiritual vacuum among the Negro people. Unquestionably, our race is now prepared, as never before, for a divine visitation. As it faces the crucial problems of the future, the race desperately needs dynamic, godly leadership. Our people wait, not only for full acceptance of their natural rights as American citizens, but, beyond this, for their spiritual rights and privileges as immortal souls. Spiritually thirsty individuals, young and old, wait to be led forth from the long Egyptian bondage of sin, fear, frustration, and uncertainty into the glorious light of redemption, freedom, and peace of Jesus Christ. How long must the Negro people wait for spiritual emancipation? The answer is largely within the province of the Negro minister.

4

The Negro and False Prophets

AS A LARGE crowd gathered on a Harlem street corner, I joined it and listened to a Negro address his attentive audience.

"I want you to know," he announced, "that I am Christ. All you have to do is believe that you are Christ and you will be Christ. You do not have to read the Bible or any other book. Too long we Negroes have been deceived by the Bible. I have been sent by God to tell you the truth."

What I saw and heard that day was disgusting. Here was another false prophet in town brainwashing the people into believing that he was some divine person, sent from God to the people. How tragic that so many people in that crowd were influenced by his words. Not knowing the truth, they fell an easy prey to his deceit.

The Bible warns about the presence of false prophets in the world. Turning to the Old Testament, in the Book of Jeremiah, we read: "Then the Lord said unto me, The prophets prophesy lies in my name: I sent them not, neither have I commanded them, neither spake unto them: they prophesy unto you a false vision and divination, and a thing of nought, and the deceit of their heart" (JEREMIAH 14:14). "Thus saith the Lord of hosts, Hearken not unto the words of the prophets that prophesy unto you: they make you vain: they speak a vision of their own heart, and not out of the mouth of the Lord" (JEREMIAH 23:16). "Behold, I am against the prophets, saith the Lord, that use their tongues, and say, He saith. Behold, I am against them that prophesy false dreams, saith the Lord, and do tell them, and cause my people to err by their lies, and by their lightness; yet I sent them not, nor commanded them: therefore they shall not profit this people at all, saith the Lord" (JEREMIAH 23:31,32).

Consider God's Word to the prophet Ezekiel: "Son of man, prophesy against the prophets of Israel that prophesy, and say thou unto them that prophesy out of their own hearts, Hear ye the word of the Lord: Thus saith the Lord God; Woe unto the foolish prophets, that follow their own spirit, and have seen nothing!" (EZEKIEL 13:2,3).

In the New Testament, Jesus Himself sounds a note of warning concerning false prophets. In His Sermon on the Mount (MATTHEW, CHAPTERS 6–8), He says: "Beware of false prophets, which come to you in sheep's clothing, but inwardly they are ravening wolves. Ye shall know them by their fruits . . ." (MATTHEW 7:15,16).

In His Olivet Discourse, our Lord mentions the presence of false prophets in the world as one of the signs of the last days. "And as he sat upon the mount of Olives, the disciples came unto him privately, saying, Tell us, when shall these things be? and what shall be the sign of thy coming, and of the end of the world? And Jesus answered and said unto them, Take heed that no man deceive you. For many shall come in my name, saying, I am Christ; and shall deceive many. . . . Then if any man shall say unto you, Lo, here is Christ, or there; believe it not. For there shall arise false Christs, and false prophets, and shall shew great signs and wonders; insomuch that, if it were possible, they shall deceive the very elect" (MATTHEW 24:3-5,23,24).

Today the number of false prophets is increasing among the Negro masses. Some of them are religious racketeers and confidence men, who build huge financial empires in terms of money and property. They ride around in chauffeur-driven limousines, wear the most expensive clothes, and live like kings in fabulous mansions. Their incredible success may be credited to their ability to capitalize on the ignorance and gullibility of ill-informed Negroes and whites.

There seem to be at least two extremes among the perpetrators of error. There are those who flatly repudiate and attack Christianity, the claims of Christ, and the Bible. The Black Muslim movement is a case in point. Then there are those who accept the Bible, but in using it twist and pervert the Scriptures so as to form their own system of theology and doctrine, doing violence to the truth of the Bible as a whole. A common practice is to lift a part of Scripture out of its context, and build a church denomination or other religious movement on it. Many church organizations exist as a result of such practice.

Various modern means of communication are used by false prophets to propagate their pseudodoctrines and religions. Travelers will observe a conglomeration of Negro religious broadcasters on radio stations from coast to coast. Most of these broadcasts are a disgrace and an embarrassment to the race as a whole. Yet many Negro churches which have the message and music to provide first-class radio programs do not avail themselves of the wonderful opportunity that radio offers for propagation of our faith. Churches and ministers with little constructive to offer, in terms of spiritual teaching and help, avail themselves of the radio dial.

The quality of many of these broadcasts is deplorable. The usual pattern is something on this order: first, a lot of spirited, jazzy singing by choirs, quartets, and soloists; then a briefing by the announcer on church news and coming events; following this there is a reading of a long list of commercial businesses which help to sponsor the broadcast (the radio listeners are strongly urged to patronize these establishments); more music is rendered; then the sermon is delivered by a bishop or prophet.

The content of the sermon itself varies. One may hear anything from black racism to a prophecy on the doom and destruction of the white race. The preacher may talk to his radio audience about one of his latest visions or dreams. He may urge his listeners to write in for his blessed handkerchiefs, roots, candles, water, oil, and other charms. Special blessings are sent to those listeners who send a contribution of one dollar or more. The larger the gift, the greater the blessing received. I heard one of these religious charlatans make the following announcement on a broadcast: "See me, ——, on Sunday and drive a Cadillac on Monday. I will bless you and you will have a happy marriage, a good job, a new home, and power over your enemies."

Another prophet offered some special floor wash to his listeners. This liquid was to keep evil spirits away from the home.

Still another said: "If you are sick and have troubles, go and get a glass of water. Put your hand on the radio. As I pray for you drink the water and all your sickness and troubles will go away."

These are but a few samples of what one hears on various Negro religious broadcasts. It would be impossible to cite all the techniques or mention the number of gimmicks false prophets use over the radio to deceive and ensnare the people.

False prophets also use the printed page to reach the masses with their message. Almost all the false cults and religions rely heavily on their tracts, magazines, newspapers, and books to advance their doctrines and beliefs.

If you scan the many Negro newspapers on sale, you will discover that a great deal of space is purchased by false prophets to advertise their services in the church section. A typical newspaper ad runs:

THOUSANDS HELPED WEEKLY BY REV. ——————
"The Highway to Success"

Don't be misled. No one man knows it all. With God's Given Power, I guarantee to do what I promise. I'll help you get and hold money. Get that new home and car. End alcoholism, crossed and unnatural conditions. Help you keep your loved one and aid in all individual problems. Weekly help. FOR "SURE, QUICK HELP," DON'T WAIT, CONTACT ME TODAY. "THROUGH GOD I DO THINGS, NOT PROMISE."

HOURS: Call after 9 P.M., Station to Station for lower rate. Sun. 10 A.M. to 5 P.M.

NO MAIL

Make one call for free information and full details. DIAL——

Television is used by cultists to bring their religious services into the homes of Negro Americans. Sometime ago I was conducting a series of meetings in a church in one of our midwestern cities. After the closing service on Sunday evening, I sat up until 1:00 a.m. to view a program conducted by one of these modern-day prophets. The prophet, dressed in a robe of splendor, sat on a throne with guards surrounding him. At a signal from him, the pianist and organist struck up a jazzy gospel song. Members in the church began to sing, shout, and dance. Emotions ran high as the people danced before the prophet. He raised his hand, a gesture that brought special blessing to the gyrating happy disciples of the movement, causing them to reach a peak of wild frenzy and hysteria.

The highlight of the whole show was the moment when the prophet offered his special cosmic prayer. A group of university students had phoned to request prayer that they receive good grades in their examinations the next day. The prophet began to work himself into a highly emotional state, trembling all over as he prayed: "O God, I ask you to bless these university students as they take their exams tomorrow. And as your servant, I command you to oil the chassis of their minds with the oil from the divine lubritorium." After the prayer, the prophet promised the students that they would be successful in passing their examinations.

Someone has said that false cults are the unpaid bills of the church. There is truth in that statement; without doubt, the church is largely responsible for the increasing number of false prophets, cults, and religions among us. The fact that so

71

many of these religious quacks continue to emerge should be a matter of grave concern to the entire Negro church. It should examine itself, see wherein it has failed, and take the necessary steps to correct its weaknesses and failures.

A noticeable point of failure is that the Negro church has not properly taught and indoctrinated its constituency in the Word of God and the doctrines of the church. As a race, we are grossly ignorant of the teachings of the Bible, even though multitudes of us have been church members for years. We do not make it a practice to read or study the Bible as God commands: "Study to shew thyself approved unto God, a workman that needeth not to be ashamed, rightly dividing the word of truth" (II TIMOTHY 2:15).

Few Negro church members carry their Bibles with them to church on Sunday. And rarely do we find a Negro church with a good supply of Bibles on hand for the convenience of the worshippers. Since very few of our Negro ministers today urge and train their parishioners to be Bible students, the people have become strangers to the Bible. Bibleless preachers in the pulpits make for Bibleless people in the pews.

Such lack of a sane and sound knowledge of the Word of God makes the Negro vulnerable to Satan's fiery darts of error and false teaching. In a climate of ignorance, fear, and superstition, false prophets exploit great numbers of Negroes for their own selfish interests. This could not happen if the Negro church were following the New Testament pattern. False prophets continue to deceive and destroy with their lies because too many of us are void of the truth. And this is exactly what the Bible teaches. "My people," God says, "are destroyed for lack of knowledge: because thou hast rejected knowledge, I will also reject thee, that thou shalt be no priest to me: seeing thou hast forgotten the law of thy God, I will also forget thy children" (HOSEA 4:6).

How can we as a people free ourselves from the false prophets and other cultists currently operating among us? How can we overcome the spread of false teaching? First, as individuals, we need to experience a personal encounter with Jesus Christ. Christ not only can free from sin but from the bondage of fear, superstition, and falsehood. By knowing Christ as Saviour and Lord, we discover that the full revelation of truth is in Jesus (EPHESIANS 4:21). Christ said: "And ye shall know the truth, and the truth shall make you free" (JOHN 8:32).

Then we must turn to the Bible, the Word of God. It is imperative that we become diligent students of the Holy Scriptures. The Bible is the greatest antidote against the deadly poison of damnable doctrines and heresies. The Bible is the Sword of the Spirit and our only sure weapon against Satan and his false prophets. As Jesus Christ used the Word of God against the attacks and temptations of Satan in the wilderness, so must we rely upon the Bible in our fight against the forces of evil and the spread of spurious teachings.

Too, we need to use the Bible to test and expose all false prophets and heresy. The Bible must be our sole authority and highest court of law as we judge the philosophies and teachings of men. We are, therefore, responsible before God to reject everything that is false and contrary to the teaching of the Word of God itself.

In the Epistle of First John we read: "Beloved, believe not every spirit, but try the spirits whether they are of God: because many false prophets are gone out into the world. Hereby know ye the Spirit of God: Every spirit that confesseth that Jesus Christ is come in the flesh is of God: And every spirit that confesseth not that Jesus Christ is come in the flesh is not of God: and this is that spirit of antichrist, whereof ye have heard that it should come; and even now already is it in the world. Ye are of God, little children, and have overcome them: because greater is he that is in you, than he that is in the world. . . . We are of God: he that knoweth God heareth us; he that is not of God heareth not us. Hereby know we the spirit of truth, and the spirit of error" (I JOHN 4:1-4,6).

And in this day of error and false teachings, we must contend for our historic Christian faith. "Contend for the faith, that was once delivered unto the saints," the Bible says. When the Negro ministers get back to the faithful teaching ministry of the Word of God, and when church members are deeply entrenched in the knowledge of Christ and the Bible, false prophets will find it extremely difficult to survive. How can these emissaries of Satan withstand the clear and compromising proclamation of the true Gospel of Jesus Christ? We do not need to be contentious in contending for the faith. Rather, in love we should proclaim the Word before all people, relying on God to use His Word to confound and defeat the prophets of deceit.

And this is of vital importance if we are to free ourselves from false prophets and false doctrines. We must not only know the Bible and contend for the truth of it, but we must personally be responsible Christians, obeying its teachings in our everyday lives. Right doctrine and right living go hand in hand. And conversely, false doctrine and false living are compatible companions. The time has come when the Negro church must produce ministers and lay members whose lives are according to the truth of the Word of God.

The Apostle Paul delivered such a challenge to the church at Corinth when he said: "Ye are our epistle written in our hearts, known and read of all men: forasmuch as ye are manifestly declared to be the epistle of Christ ministered by us, written not with ink, but with the Spirit of the living God: not in tables of stone, but in fleshly tables of the heart. And such trust have we through Christ to God-ward: Not that we are sufficient of ourselves to think any thing as of ourselves; but our sufficiency is of God" (II CORINTHIANS 3:2-5).

Yes, false prophets have arisen among us. The Negro race, unfortunately, has produced its Father Divines, Daddy Graces, Elijah Muhammads, and other false christs and prophets. Multitudes of deceived and deluded souls like blind sheep follow their pernicious ways. How patient is God! How merciful and long-suffering is He to tolerate the foolishness of these brazen religious leaders, who habitually flout themselves before Him in their sins and hypocrisy. God is not asleep. He is mindful of all things. The Bible reveals that God has ordained a day when He will judge Satan and all his false prophets. The God of Truth and His Son, Jesus Christ, will vindicate themselves of everything that is false and deceitful among men.

As Negroes, we should cleanse ourselves of all hypocrisy and live "soberly, righteously, and godly in this present world." It is necessary for us to expose, denounce, and reject all false prophets, with their lies, dreams, and visions. Our true Saviour and Prophet is Jesus Christ, the Son of God. He is the Christ of Calvary, whose nail-scarred hands point us in the way of righteousness, purity, honesty, truth, and in the end, eternal life. With complete confidence in Him we can sing:

> "Glory, glory, hallelujah!
> His truth is marching on."

5

The Supreme Task of the Negro Church

CERTAIN ANALOGIES MAY be drawn between the early years of the first century and our own. Outwardly it was a splendid age in which, under Roman rule, the modern "one world" concept seemed to have been realized. The arts and sciences were highly developed. Commercial and military travel were made easy by splendidly kept roads which extended to the farthest confines of the empire. Caravans were constantly traversing the area which was midway between the eastern and western extremities—Palestine, locale of the ministry of our Lord. One language—Greek—speeded the exchange of ideas.

But internal conditions, those of the spirit, were bad. The old philosophies and religions had a tired look. The temples fostered all sorts of evils. Seneca, the great Roman philosopher, wrote: "All things are full of crimes and vices." The Apostle Paul agreed with this when he described conditions in ROMANS 1:18-32. Human life was lightly esteemed; it was sacrificed daily for the people's pleasure in the circus exhibitions. Slavery cursed the empire.

The Gospel proclaimed by our Lord was characterized by a reawakening of the religious sense. It presented an adequate object of worship. It insisted on purity in moral conduct. It emphasized the value of human life. It preached a faith and hope which rejuvenated the hearts of men. So well did the message proclaimed by its Founder work, that within thirty

77

years after the Gospel began to be preached by the church there were great numbers of Christians. Within three centuries the Roman empire succumbed to its influence, purged by the purifying "waters" of the Word.

Before His Ascension Jesus turned over the "keys of the kingdom" to His followers. With His help they could open doors no man could shut. They were to continue His program, depending on His Spirit and availing themselves of His presence. They were to adopt His method and use it as a pattern.

". . . Go ye into all the world, and preach the gospel to every creature" (MARK 16:15) were His parting instructions. When the church has obeyed these instructions, it has prospered. When it has forsaken them, dark ages have settled on it like a shroud.

These words, which we have come to call "The Great Commission," have been a challenge to my own heart and ministry. They seemed to say to me that my choice as a Christian minister and disciple of Christ was not only between the evil and the good, but between the good and the best. Surely there were evils rampant in the Roman empire, but about them Jesus and St. Paul had little to say. By going to the heart of the matter, the transformation of human character, the Gospel they preached would eventually work a miracle in the body politic.

The fact that The Commission was practically the closing message of our Lord emphasizes its importance. Last words are carefully weighed. With what was it primarily concerned? Evangelism and worldwide missions. Doubtless there were many words of wisdom Jesus in those closing hours would liked to have shared with His disciples. But He concentrated upon the work to which the Father had commissioned Him. Now that He was leaving them, they were to continue His work.

What did Jesus consider the supreme task of the church to be? What weighed most upon His heart? Not universal suffrage, improved living conditions, nor political and social reform. Not the establishment of humanitarian agencies, nor foundations and other enterprises for various charities. Not a word did He say about civil rights! Instead, He defined the supreme task of the church to be the evangelization of the whole world through the proclamation of His Gospel.

When we examine the Negro churches of our day, we find them sadly lacking in vision for evangelism and worldwide missions. While there are a few churches across the country that are engaged in such a program, the majority are absolutely blind to the need for a soul-winning ministry on a local and worldwide basis. Our churches are involved in almost every task except the supreme one of evangelizing the world, in obedience to the command of Christ! Evangelism and missions have little or no place on the agenda of most churches. What a shame and disgrace before God!

The Negro church in America needs to understand that God has a primary program for His Church, and that is the program of evangelism and worldwide missions. We have lost sight of this. Instead, most churches are overloaded with programs which God has never ordained or endorsed. The average church is programed to death. Its church leaders spend their strength in devising new undertakings for the church that will work like magic to attract more people and increase the flow of money into the treasury. This largely explains why our churches at times actually compete with one another on the basis of church programs and clubs, the thought being that the more programs and clubs a church has, the more valuable that church is in terms of service to the community.

If Jesus Christ, the Supreme and Sovereign Head of the church, should visit one of our Sunday morning worship services, He would undoubtedly effect drastic and revolutionary changes, as in the temple of old. He would overturn many things and cleanse the precincts. He would cast out our man-made programs and dissolve the legion of social and other worldly clubs we have embraced. Then He would challenge

79

these churches by saying: "I have only one real program for My church, and that is the program of evangelism and world-wide missions."

Certain reasons may be discerned why most Negro churches today lack a vision for missions. To a great extent it is charge-able to the leadership in the church. We have ministers with-out vision, and the Bible says: "Where there is no vision, the people perish . . ." (PROVERBS 29:18). A visionless pastor makes for a visionless church, and both the pastor and the church suffer.

Then, too, a large percentage of trained and qualified Negro ministers were not taught the importance of evangelism and missions during their college and seminary training. They have never really been challenged with the supreme task of the church. Because of racism, many of these men were not welcomed as students in the white evangelical Bible schools, colleges, and seminaries where the Bible is taught, expounded, and accepted as the infallible Word of Almighty God and where evangelism and missions are set forth as the primary concern of the Christian church. As a consequence, these men were forced to obtain their training in liberal institutions where the historic Gospel of the cross and the urgent need to evangelize lost mankind with that Gospel seem forgotten. They graduated with hearts cold and indifferent to the su-preme task of the church.

How can we expect such ministers to bring a vision for missions to their churches? This is a most unfortunate situa-tion, and on this particular point white evangelicals must as-sume the blame. Failure to give Negro ministers the opportu-nity to be exposed to the message of evangelism and missions left Negro clergymen in the darkness of ignorance. As of now, some white evangelical schools accept Negroes as students, but the number is still too small. Wherever a Negro church is found to be on fire for missions, the cause may usually be traced to the training its pastor has received.

Another reason why Negro churches lack a real vision for

evangelism and missions is that many of the outstanding Negro ministers tend to be selfish. They labor hard and long to build huge religious empires which they themselves control within the four walls of their own church and denomination. And apart from the current civil-rights and other social and political commitments, it is difficult and sometimes impossible to get these ministers interested in any evangelistic and missionary program, whether it be at home or abroad. They are totally unconcerned about a crusade that is dedicated to the sole purpose of bringing lost men and women to the Saviour. At times some of these ministers will support a soul-saving effort, but only if they are given places of prominence and authority. It is not unusual for some to ask: "What is there in this for me? Will I get any money for my services?" A selfish minister is definitely void of missionary passion. The ministry of evangelism and missions is for the spiritual benefit and blessing of others. In it, selfishness should have no place.

The time has come when Negro churches in America must awake and accept responsibility for worldwide missions. They must have a vision of the home and foreign field. With John Wesley the Negro church must say "the whole world is my parish"; it must be realized that The Great Commission of Jesus Christ is not only a positive command to white churches, but to the Negro churches as well. The Negro church must become involved in evangelism and missions if it is to fulfill its high calling.

Such involvement would obligate the Negro church to send forth more of its own qualified missionaries into the world. These missionaries must first have experienced the transforming power of the grace of God in their own lives, and be able to meet every other requirement for missionaries in this fast-changing space age.

As an evangelist who spends a great deal of time each year in evangelistic work in Africa, I observe large numbers of white young men and women coming from America and Europe to do missionary work. In obedience to Christ's "Go ye,"

81

these young people leave their loved ones and the comforts of home and their churches. They make many sacrifices, exposing themselves to an enervating climate, disease, fever, danger, and frustrating circumstances. If necessary, they are prepared to become martyrs for the advancement of the cause of Christ on earth. But it is usually a steady, unending stream of white missionary recruits. Very few Negroes are among them, and most of these are women. We are deeply grateful for these faithful servants of Christ; they are doing a tremendous job. But why are the Negro missionaries so few in number?

When I return to the United States and minister in various Negro churches, I see multitudes of fine young people in the congregations. What tremendous missionary material! Many of them are working hard for the Lord, but they don't realize that a far richer ministry for Christ is open to them in Africa and other countries. On the mission fields abroad they could reach those Christless masses who sit in spiritual darkness, pleading like a certain Arab sheik:

> "And still I wait
> For the messenger of Christ
> Who cometh late."

What a thrill these young people would experience in serving as ambassadors for Christ and sharing the Gospel of our crucified and risen Lord with those who have never had the opportunity of hearing it.

The prophet Isaiah one day caught a vision of the Lord upon His throne. This vision of God's holiness caused the prophet to confess his sins and then receive spiritual cleansing. Following this he received a commission from the Lord for divine service. Speaking of this commission, the prophet says: "Also I heard the voice of the Lord, saying, Whom shall I send, and who will go for us? Then said I, Here am I; send me. And he said, Go, and tell this people . . ." (ISAIAH 6:8, 9).

God continues to summon laborers for His vineyard. But

how many Negro Christians today will respond to this divine call, as did Isaiah centuries ago? We say we love the Lord, and in church we sing lustily, "Where He leads me I will follow," but we really do not mean it. If we did, more Negroes would find themselves in Christian work in the regions beyond. The fact is that many are so entrenched in material things that they have little time to invest in the Lord's work. They are not willing to pioneer and make sacrifices for Christ; neither are they spiritually prepared to pay the price for real discipleship. Too long Negro Christians have sat idly by and let the white man pioneer new mission fields and assume the greater part of the responsibility for world evangelism. Now Negroes must see their own responsibility, and do their part in helping to evangelize the world for our Lord. The Negro churches need to improve their spiritual condition if they are to give birth to missionary sons and daughters. What a testimony it would be for a great army of dedicated and trained young Negro men and women to go forth for service on the mission fields around the world. Under the banner of the cross of Christ, with the Bible in their hands and the love of Christ in their hearts, these young people could march as Christian soldiers and demonstrate their deep compassion and love for lost sinners by winning them to the Saviour, Jesus Christ.

A church that puts evangelism and missions first and sends out missionaries to the fields abroad is a church in the divine order, one that can claim the blessing of God and be filled with spiritual life and power. Conversely, a church without a vision and one that does not establish Christian witnesses in places beyond its own home base is a dead church, regardless of how large or wealthy it may be. Let the Negro church today scrap the many Christ-dishonoring and time-consuming programs of men, and get wholly involved in God's great program of worldwide missions and evangelism while there is still time. Then it can be said, as Paul said of the church at Thessalonica: ". . . ye were ensamples to all that believe in Macedonia and Achaia. For from you sounded out the word of the Lord not only in Macedonia and Achaia, but also in every place your faith to God-ward is spread abroad . . ." (I THESSALONIANS 1:7,8).

Involvement in the work of The Great Commission also entails a financial responsibility for the support of the ministry of evangelism and missions. The Bible has a great deal to say on the subject of Christian stewardship. It is the will of God that Christians abound in the grace of giving. God has a claim upon us and upon all that we possess in this world. Everything in heaven and on earth belongs to God, as He says: "For every beast of the forest is mine, and the cattle upon a thousand hills. I know all the fowls of the mountains: and the wild beasts of the field are mine. If I were hungry, I would not tell thee: for the world is mine, and the fulness thereof" (PSALM 50:10-12). "The silver is mine, and the gold is mine, saith the Lord of hosts" (HAGGAI 2:8).

"We have become accustomed to talking," says Dr. Robert Hall Glover, "in terms of ownership of property and personal effects, but in reality no man owns anything. We simply have the use of what we call our possessions, for the brief term of our earthly life at longest, and then we must relinquish them all! 'For we brought nothing into this world, and it is certain we can carry nothing out' (I TIMOTHY 6:7). It is fundamental to a right understanding of stewardship that we realize and accept this great fact. Only by the favor of Almighty God do we possess anything, and He can take it from us at any moment that He chooses to do so."

Negro Christians need a right understanding of stewardship. We are failing God in our giving, especially when it comes to the support of missions. The average Negro church gives very little money towards the work of evangelism and worldwide missions. The church that gives substantially is an exceptional one. Missionary giving in Negro churches is not in accordance with the ability to give. The potential is there, but the vision and the willingness are sadly lacking.

How does one explain this situation? First blame must be

placed on the ministers. If we are correct in saying that the majority of Negro ministers have no vision for evangelism and missions, it is quite understandable why their churches are pitifully weak in giving liberally to missionary enterprises. The Negro minister is the leader of his people, and his enthusiasm or lack of it for any financial project in the church can either spell success or failure. For example, it is quite easy to get Negro ministers interested in raising large sums of money for their church building programs. No minister hesitates to ask for an increased salary or a better parsonage in which to live. Consider how zealously many Negro ministers raise thousands of dollars for the civil-rights movement and other humanitarian or charitable causes. These men are successful money-raisers because these are projects in which they are deeply interested.

How many of these ministers would exercise the same zeal and enthusiasm in raising comparable sums of money for evangelism and missions? They have a vision for money for material things and for those objects that relate to their own interests, but where is their vision for the money that is so desperately needed to save the immortal souls of men?

Local church disputes and splits often hinder the increase of missionary giving. This fact also holds true for denominations and church conventions. People cannot be expected to be united in giving for a cause if they are divided in spirit.

In talking with Negro ministers, missionaries, and lay Christians, I find that many are discouraged and refuse to give to the foreign-missions department of their denominations because of instances where there have been misappropriations of funds by some mission officials.

One Negro minister in Detroit expressed his feelings this way: "In our church we are willing to do more for missions. We must do more than we have been doing. But we are tired of all the wrangling that is going on in our denomination. And we know that some of the money our churches give to missions through our Convention never gets to the missionaries on the field. We have decided, therefore, not to give any more mission money through the regular channels. We now want to give it directly to our missionaries on the field and then we know it will get there and be used for the purpose given."

A Negro missionary in Africa said: "During my last furlough in the States I told my friends that if they had any money they wanted to give to help me in my missionary work that they had better send it to me on the field so that I would be sure to receive it. I have had experiences where money was given for me and I never received it."

It is extremely necessary for the Negro church in this crisis hour to abound in the ministry of Christian stewardship. Currently the offering accompanied by the greatest noise in our churches is the missionary offering taken each month on missionary Sunday. One can hear the jingling of pennies, nickels, dimes, and quarters which the affluent Negro worshippers drop into the collection plates. "Brethren, these things ought not so to be." It is going to take more than coins to evangelize this hell-bound world of ours. In the spirit of sacrifice we must give thousands of dollars each year if the Negro church is to effectively conduct its ministry of evangelism, both at home and abroad.

Again quoting that reverend missionary statesman, Dr. Robert H. Glover: "The completion of the task of world-evangelization within the present generation is, we claim, sanely practicable through a Church that will measure up to God's conditions. But it will never be achieved without sacrifice, and that for the simple reason that God never intended it to be. He who laid the foundation of the enterprise in the sacrifice of His well-beloved Son will have it continued and finished only by sacrificial means. Sacrifice is the very soul of missions. The high cost to those who have gone to the front is clearly apparent, as expressed in arduous toil, patient endurance and in many cases martyr death. But God has not different standards for those who go and those who stay. The latter

86

are expected to manifest the same degree of consecration and make as great sacrifices as those who go. The red tinge of sacrifice should be upon everyone's share in this great work for Christ, wherever and whatever one's part may be. It is that which gives all service for Him its value. But after Calvary what is worthy to be called sacrifice? Can anything be deemed too costly to give to Jesus Christ?"

Not long ago a Negro Christian woman in Texas listened to one of her daily religious broadcasts. She heard the announcement that a missionary radio station in Monrovia, Liberia, had opened a financial drive for a new hospital. She was eighty years of age and a widow, but God spoke to her. For many years she had been interested in missions in Liberia, and had wanted to do something for the Lord in that country. After a few days of prayer, she decided to sell some of the property her husband left her. In time it was sold, and she sent a check for $10,000 to Radio Station ELWA for the construction of one of the hospital wings, and later gave another $5,000 to furnish the new hospital addition. We need more of this spirit of giving among our people. Poverty-stricken giving to missions has brought a reproach on the name of Christ and a curse to our Negro missionaries on the foreign field.

In my ministry on Negro mission stations in Liberia and other parts of Africa, I have found most of these stations to be understaffed and insufficiently financed, due to lack of support by churches in the States. Some of our missionaries barely have enough money to buy food and take care of their most pressing needs. The homes in which some missionaries live are dilapidated and are without water, electricity, and proper sanitary facilities. Mission churches, schools, and clinics are far from adequate to meet the challenge of the spiritual, educational, and medical needs of the African people. Is it fair that Negro church leaders and other Christians at home should live so comfortably and even in luxury, while their missionaries suffer? Where is the love of God manifested when such deplorable conditions are permitted to exist?

Once in a large church meeting in Cleveland, Ohio, I listened to an African government official challenge the Negro ministers and other Christian workers to do more in the way of giving money for missions so that their mission stations in his country might be brought up to the standards of other well-established missions. His message was a stinging rebuke, and it was a shame that he had to give it.

The Negro church must rise to its financial obligation. Let our churches abound in the giving of tithes and offerings for the work of the Lord. Yes, let the Negro ministers set an example by sacrificing some of the "special days" which their churches designate each year for the showering of money, expensive cars, and other costly gifts on them. If our ministers would make such a sacrifice for the Lord, their churches would be better able to give more money to missions.

Certainly a church is responsible before God to support its minister so that he can take care of his family, keep out of debt, and give his full time to the ministry, and thereby render a real spiritual service to his church. ". . . the labourer is worthy of his hire . . ." (LUKE 10:7).

But in many cases ministers expect entirely too much in the way of financial returns and other benefits. What a church does for its minister should be more in proportion; it is quite evident that far too many "men of the cloth" are financially exploiting their churches for their own gain. These men live on a level far too high above that of their congregations, and such plush living brings the ministry under fire from the critics who believe that the Negro ministry has deteriorated into a profitable racket for those who want an easy living.

God is ready to bless the Negro communion if it will put His program of evangelism and missions first and support that program with its tithes and offerings. What a privilege we have as Christians to invest in the greatest business on earth—that sacred one of bringing the glorious Gospel to lost sinners of every race and nationality. The dollars we invest in this cause bring both earthly and eternal blessings and rewards from the hand of God. God is calling Negro churches to a greater dedication to the ministry of Christian stewardship. The questions of an ancient, honored prophet should be carefully asked by each of us! "Will a man rob God? Yet ye have robbed me. But ye say, Wherein have we robbed thee? In tithes and offerings. Ye are cursed with a curse: for ye have robbed me, even this whole nation. Bring ye all the tithes into the storehouse, that there may be meat in mine house, and prove me now herewith, saith the Lord of hosts, if I will not open you the windows of heaven, and pour you out a blessing, that there shall not be room enough to receive it" (MALACHI 3:8-10).

In the New Testament we read: ". . . He which soweth sparingly shall reap also sparingly; and he which soweth bountifully shall reap also bountifully. Every man according as he purposeth in his heart, so let him give; not grudgingly, or of necessity: for God loveth a cheerful giver" (II CORINTHIANS 9:6,7).

The Negro church has a responsibility to pray fervently for the work of evangelism and missions. Great exploits are accomplished by God on the mission field when Christians at home are on their knees in prayer. A prayerless church is guilty of sin before God, for the ministry of missions and evangelism is thereby hindered and Satan claims a victory.

In these days of uncertainty, tension, and turmoil the world over, missionaries need our prayer support as never before. On the field they are constantly placed in frustrating circumstances as they labor to advance the cause of Christ and the Gospel. Often they feel the crushing pressures and fierce attacks of the devil working against them. They are plagued by loneliness, discouragement, depression, and despair. At times they become incapacitated and handicapped by illness. Some experience a complete physical and mental breakdown and have to return home. And there are those worthy soldiers of the cross who are called upon to lay down their lives for Christ and the souls of men. A missionary's life is not glamorous, nor

89

is it easy. Real courage and dedication are required of those who go to the regions beyond. This is why it is so essential that we bathe our missionaries in prayer. Pray that God will bless, encourage, strengthen, and protect them as they blaze pioneer trails for the Gospel.

The Negro church must pray fervently that the Lord will send forth more Negro missionaries to the fields. God knows and we know that more missionary recruits are needed. How shall we get them? We have the answer to that question in the words of our Lord: ". . . The harvest truly is plenteous, but the labourers are few; Pray ye therefore the Lord of the harvest, that he will send forth labourers into his harvest" (MATTHEW 9:37,38).

"The labourers are few!" How true this is of conditions in the Negro church relative to securing better qualified missionary personnel to meet the call of the "regions beyond." How tragic it is that so many of our young people remain at home, and so few are willing to respond to the "Macedonian Call." Yet we have the opportunity to lay this problem in prayer before our Lord. He is the Lord of the harvest—the mission fields of the whole world belong to Him. And He has made Himself responsible for the supply of labourers for His harvest. As the Negro church assumes a greater portion of the burden of prayer for missions, our Lord will lay His hands upon young men and women in our churches and thrust them out into the fields. God help us, therefore, to pray for more dedicated Christian workers. Too long there has been "ease in Zion." The church must bring forth children who will represent her abroad and bring honor and glory to Jesus Christ.

There are a few relatively simple things that Negro churches may do to inspire and maintain the spirit of missions and evangelism.

Each year a missionary convention should be held in the churches. The length of such a convention might run from one day to a week, but no longer. Both Negro and white missionaries at home on furlough should be invited as speakers. They should be given ample time to unburden their souls and show pictures of their work.

A missionary panel could be set up so that people attending a convention might ask questions and receive authoritative information.

Missionaries should make available to the people the finest of missionary literature, much of which can be obtained free from the various missionary societies. Missionary biographies and other books dealing with evangelism could be sold to the people or made available through church libraries.

In every service the opportunity should be given to young people to offer their lives for Christian service. Those who respond must be instructed on the importance of being fully trained for the Lord's work.

During the missionary convention a special offering should be taken. From the very beginning the pastor should inform his people about the offering so that they will be fully prepared to give a generous offering, generally on the last day of the meetings. This money should be used to support the work of the missionary abroad. The churches should be encouraged to increase their missionary giving each year. Such a procedure would help to keep missions and evangelism in the thoughts of the people. It would also help to enforce the commitment of a continuing financial obligation.

In most Negro churches the establishment of a mission would have to begin in a small way. The fact is that this must be started, and the time is now. The Negro church is at the crossroads. It will either experience a mighty spiritual revival and become involved in the ministry of evangelism, or it will eventually die. The Negro church cannot remain in its status quo. It must be a question of life or death, going forward or backward. God calls the church to its supreme task of reaching men with the Gospel of Jesus Christ. A church involved in God's program is sure to overcome its enemies and its trials, for Christ said: ". . . upon this rock I will build my church; and the gates of hell shall not prevail against it" (MATTHEW 16:18).

6

Should More Negro Missionaries Be Used?

SEVERAL YEARS AGO at the conclusion of a missionary meeting in Cleveland, Ohio, one of the speakers, a white lady missionary from Africa, raised a common question: "Howard, as pastor of this church, I know you have a real burden in the evangelization of your people both here in America and in Africa. God is blessing your radio ministry here and abroad. However, it is my opinion that your proposal to visit Africa personally for evangelistic work is good but not practical."

"Why?" I asked, although I was acquainted with the argument.

"Because the Africans will not accept the Gospel from you as a Negro as they accept it from us," was the sincere reply. "You see, Africans would resent your coming to tell them about Jesus Christ and their need of salvation because they consider themselves on the same plane as yourself. They would expect you to dress, eat, and live as they do, and if you should refuse there would be offense. But with the white missionary it is different because we are from another race and culture."

I could not accept this missionary's appraisal of the situation. I had heard this line of reasoning from other white missionaries, mission officials, and once from a Bible professor. I disagreed with her as I did with others, feeling that she was biased in her attitude toward the use of Negro missionaries in Africa or anywhere else in the world. All meant well, I felt sure, but I was certain they were ignorant of certain facts.

There was only one thing for me to do—namely, to visit the mission fields of Africa and gain firsthand experience for myself.

God was blessing our radio ministry each week across the continent of Africa, over radio station ELWA in Monrovia, Liberia, West Africa. From this country I was sending my taped messages abroad. Thousands of Africans listened regularly to my messages from the Word of God. From announcements on the broadcasts they knew that I was an American Negro, and the music presented was that of a Negro church. But how would my African listeners react toward me if I came to visit them? Would I be accepted as their brother from America or rejected? A personal visit to Africa, I reasoned, would provide the answer.

The statement by my missionary friend accomplished one good purpose. It caused me to do some research on the history of Negro missionaries on the mission fields of the world. Zealously I turned to books, and conversed with missionaries and mission officials of various denominations. The information I received was heartwarming. Negro missionaries in the past had made a tremendous contribution to the foreign field. Such was the written record. But it was not one easily to be found on the surface. I had to search for it as for hidden treasure.

A Southern Baptist publication, *The Baptist Advance,* directed my attention to one, Rev. George Lisle, a Baptist preacher born in Virginia about 1750. Under the searching words of Rev. Matthew Moore, Lisle was converted and by him baptized. The *Advance* says that in time Lisle became a legend, and that his name should rank with such missionary pioneers as William Carey, Adoniram Judson, Robert Morrison, Robert Moffat, David Livingstone, and others. In fact, Lisle preceded all the above-named in missionary service.

Lisle married early, and into his home were born three sons and a daughter. He was a slave, but one who fortunately had an understanding, magnanimous master. Recognizing Lisle's gifts, the master set him free so that he might devote himself to

94

preaching. A man's gift "maketh him room," regardless of color, and soon Lisle was preaching in the back country along the Savannah River, and at times to the white church where he held membership. When the British occupied the Savannah area, Lisle and some of the members from the rural district sought refuge in the city, where they founded the First Negro Baptist Church in Savannah.

The war over, Lisle went to Jamaica, British West Indies, as an indentured servant of Col. Kirkland, who had been the chief British occupation officer of Savannah. Col. Kirkland had rescued Lisle from prison when the Sharp family attempted to reenslave him.

Lisle reached Kingston in 1783, and at the recommendation of Col. Kirkland was employed by the governor of Jamaica, Gen. Campbell. Working hard and living frugally, Lisle was able to obtain his certificate of manumission the following year. Four men who had emigrated from the American colonies joined him in Kingston, and with them he founded the first Negro Baptist church on the Island. Lisle proved to be a fiery preacher, and his words were too hot for the established Church of England. Opposition and persecution followed. Services were interrupted, and eventually there was imprisonment. The charge against him and his fellows was sedition, a capital offense under the law. Lisle escaped the death penalty, but a preacher companion was hanged.

Like the bold apostles Peter and John, this servant of Christ returned to his calling when he was freed from prison. Within a few years his church grew to a membership of 500 and spread into the outlying districts. Men of influence, like Steven A. Cook, who solicited funds in England, came to his aid, and enough money was raised for a permanent church edifice.

Besides a warm heart and flaming words, Lisle possessed other gifts: a fair education, tact, and the ability to lead. And he was conscious of the fact that he was part of a larger world. In 1842 more than 50 missionaries were sent from his church for missionary work in Africa. There were many "firsts" to his

95

credit: first ordained Negro preacher in America, so far as is known, first Negro missionary on record, and first of his race to send missionaries back to the land of his origin.

Another early pioneer Negro missionary was Lott Carey, who earned his freedom from slavery in 1813 and entered the Gospel ministry. Mindful of the land from which he came, he determined to return there with the light of the Gospel. But what would he use for money? Others must see the need if he was to go. He spent several years with the colored segment of the First Baptist Church of Richmond, Virginia, gaining their support. Then, with Collin Teague as co-worker, in 1821 he sailed to Liberia with the blessing of the Triennial Convention at Richmond and a colonization society that was assisting free Negroes to return to Liberia.

As time passed Negro missionaries from various denominations were sent to Africa, Haiti, and Jamaica. During the years 1820–1890, we read of the ministry of Daniel Coker (African Methodist), Scipio Beanes (African Methodist Episcopal), Henry Garnett (Presbyterian), Joshua Day, A. I. Jones, T. J. Bowen, and Henry Goodall (Southern Baptist), and W. H. Sheppard (Southern Presbyterian).

From the ranks of The Christian and Missionary Alliance the following Negro missionaries went to Sierra Leone, West Africa, during 1913–1938: Miss Carrie E. Merriweather, Rev. and Mrs. Eugene N. Thornley, Rev. and Mrs. Montrose A. Waite, Rev. and Mrs. Raymond H. Wilson, and Miss Anita Bolden. This list is by no means exhaustive. But enough have been mentioned to establish the fact that Negro missionaries have throughout the years made a distinct contribution to foreign missionary work. God blessed their labors, and though most of those mentioned have now passed from the earthly scene, "their works do follow them."

Today in this modern space age missionaries continue to serve the Lord on various fields, servants of Christ representing many churches, denominations, and interdenominational faith missions. In Liberia, for example, one sees the excellent missionary work American Negroes are doing. There is the Suehn Industrial Mission, sponsored by the National Baptist Convention, U.S.A., Inc. For over forty years Mrs. Mattie Mae Davis has directed the work of this mission, one of the oldest in the country. "Mother Mae," as she is affectionately known by the people of Liberia, continues the work of missions and evangelism.

To this may be added the Lott Carey Mission, Carver Foreign Mission, Killingsworth Mission, Afro-American Mission, United Holy Church of America Mission, and those conducted by the Presbyterians, Episcopalians, Methodists, and others.

Liberia has a larger percentage of American Negro missionaries than any other foreign country. This does not mean that Liberia's spiritual needs are greater than those of other countries. But it does have some significance when we realize that it was the freed Negro slaves from America who returned home to establish the Republic of Liberia on the West Coast of Africa. Today, the bonds of understanding and friendship are close between America and Liberia. Liberia's "Open Door Policy," formulated by the president, Dr. William V. S. Tubman, serves not only for the economic and industrial prosperity and development of the country, but also exists for the spiritual welfare of the Liberian people through the church and the ministry of evangelism and Christian missions. American Negro and white missionaries appreciate the many opportunities they have to witness for Christ in Liberia. This country is unique for the work of the Lord. President Tubman realizes the worth of Christian missionaries, and this can also be said for the vice-president, Dr. William R. Tolbert. This open door to the Gospel that one finds in Liberia and the close proximity of the people to the American way of life explain to some extent why more American Negro missionaries are laboring there than anywhere else.

Negro missionaries are currently working in Ghana, Nigeria, the Congo, Sudan, and in parts of East Africa and other places on the African continent. But we must not get the impression that the ministry of Negro missionaries today is confined to Africa. Recently, Miss Eileen H. Murray was sent to South India by the Lutheran Church as a missionary teacher.

During a recent visit to Jamaica, West Indies, for a series of evangelistic meetings, I observed the fine missionary work of Rev. and Mrs. James Massey. Rev. Massey took a three-years' leave from his church in Detroit to supervise the mission work of his denomination in Jamaica.

In Brazil, Rev. Samuel Durant is laboring for Jesus Christ and the Gospel. Likely there are other countries unknown to me where Negro missionaries are serving.

How do the nationals react to the ministry of Negro missionaries in their countries? Are Negro missionaries generally accepted or rejected by the people to whom they minister? The truth is that in all cases I have studied, Negro missionaries are well received by the nationals. The missionaries themselves are enthusiastic about the ministry God has given them. The fact that they are Negro missionaries in a foreign country has not hindered their ministry, but rather enhanced it. Certainly this has been the case in my ministry in Africa and other parts of the world.

In January, 1957, at the invitation of radio station ELWA, the radio voice of the Sudan Interior Mission, my wife and I went to West Africa for a series of evangelistic crusades in Liberia, Ghana, and Nigeria. We were thrilled with the opportunity to carry the Gospel to the people on that continent. This visit came as a result of God's blessing on our weekly broadcasts over ELWA to Africa.

I shall never forget the wonderful reception we received from the Liberian people. Members of government and people from all walks of life enthusiastically welcomed us. Our first meetings were held in the beautiful Centennial Pavilion in the capitol city of Monrovia, where in one week thousands gathered to hear the good news of the Gospel. God blessed His Word, and five hundred decisions were recorded. As a follow-up program for the new converts, a Youth for Christ organization was formed. This youth meeting still functions every Saturday evening, and not long ago it became a member of Youth For Christ International.

While in the city of Monrovia we were cordially greeted by the illustrious president of Liberia, Dr. William V. S. Tubman. President and Mrs. Tubman tendered a state luncheon in our honor, during which the President expressed his joy at our presence in his country as messengers of the Word of God.

From Monrovia our tour reached the interior of Liberia; at one place hundreds of people came running toward us. They sang, chanted, and spoke in their native language. The sound of African drums pierced our ears. My wife and I were a little nervous about this unusual reception because the people kept crowding around us. Some stretched forth their hands to touch us. Their friendly smiles greeted us. I turned to an accompanying missionary to ask the meaning.

"Oh," was the reply, "don't be nervous. This is the way the people respond when visitors come to this country. In their native language they are praising God for the fact that He has brought their colored brother and sister from America to tell them about Jesus Christ."

The missionary continued: "Some of them are saying that for two years they have listened to your voice over the radio and now they have the privilege of looking into your face for the first time. They are thrilled to know that you are in Liberia. They consider you to be not only a brother in the flesh, but as one in Christ."

Such an experience naturally moved us deeply.

From Liberia we journeyed to Ghana. Again God gave many wonderful opportunities to proclaim the Word of God; thousands heard the Word, and hundreds responded to the call of Christ.

Two Ghanaian policemen met me one day, and one asked, "Pardon me, Sir, are you an American Negro?"

"Yes, I am," I replied.

"Let me shake your hand," the policeman remarked. "This is the first time we have ever seen an American Negro, and we welcome you to our country."

Nigeria, with the largest population on the continent, also afforded a marvelous opportunity in crusades to preach and testify to the saving grace of God. In answer to prayer, hundreds found new life in Christ.

One Nigerian was so overjoyed at our visit that he wept and said: "This is the first time I have seen a Negro preacher. For years the white missionaries have come to tell us about Jesus Christ. But now we are proud to have you in Nigeria. You are one of us."

One morning I spoke to a group of Nigerian students at a mission school. Upon arrival I found a large classroom filled to capacity with 600 boys and girls. On the bulletin board the teacher had written a word of greeting: "Welcome Pastor and Mrs. Howard O. Jones to Africa—the Fatherland."

During this tour in Liberia, Ghana, and Nigeria I had an opportunity to talk freely with African Christians on a wide range of subjects. Once in the city of Lagos, Nigeria, I spoke to a group of Christian journalists. One of the men said: "Pastor Jones, we certainly appreciate your visit to us here in Nigeria. We have been regular listeners to your broadcasts for a long time, and now we are so happy that God has brought you and Mrs. Jones to us. But why have we not seen more Negro missionaries in Africa? We appreciate the ministry of our white brethren, but where are the Negro missionaries? Really, you are the first Negro preacher that some of us have ever seen or heard.

"We have been told," the man continued, "that in America there are large Negro churches with outstanding ministers and choirs, and that the Negro people are very religious. It is a mystery to us why they don't come and tell us about Jesus Christ and help us as we labor to build Africa."

After a moment of reflection I replied: "Well, my friends, for many years our Negro young people in America have

100

wanted to come to Africa for missionary work, but they were told by some white missionaries that if they came you would not receive the Gospel from them as you do from the whites. So many American Negroes thought it best not to come."

"That is not so, that is not so," said one of the men. "We do want more American Negroes serving in Africa as missionaries, and we cannot understand why white missionaries would tell you such a thing."

I could see that these African men were upset over my observation. "Have you ever asked white missionaries why more American Negroes have not come to Africa as missionaries?" I asked.

"Yes," remarked the Africans.

"Well, what did they say?"

"Oh, they told us that you all could come if you wanted to, but that you were not really interested in us," replied one African.

Unquestionably, our conversation indicated the insincerity of some white missionaries. Their fabrications or wrong deductions served to widen the gulf between Africans and American Negroes, and made proper understanding and communication difficult. Because of this separation, American Negroes were also deprived of their inalienable right before God to render missionary service in the regions abroad.

At the beginning of our African tour we worked with several white missionary societies. Many missionaries and mission officials were apprehensive about our ministry in Africa, especially those from the south in the United States. These people had never been associated with American Negroes in missionary work, and now we were all brought together for the first time. A few missionaries were quite open and frank in discussing the race problem with us. Some were very happy about our coming and pledged their support in prayer and for any help and assistance that they might be able to give. Others, however, unashamedly admitted they did not believe any American Negro evangelist or missionary could have an effective ministry among the Africans—that is, a ministry comparable to that of the whites. Consequently these missionaries considered our ministry in Africa as "the SIM (Sudan Interior Mission) experiment."

But as time passed, God put His seal of endorsement upon our ministry. In this movement of spiritual blessing, many preconceived ideas and prejudices of the whites melted away. They saw that God could use a Negro as well as a white person in Christian service. Africans recognized this also, and expressed their great desire that more American Negroes would come to Africa for Christian service.

We left Nigeria in April, 1957, with mixed emotions. We praised God for the rich experiences He had granted. We had been pioneers in more ways than one, and the task had not been easy. However, God infused a great love and appreciation in our hearts for the people of Africa. They had graciously reciprocated this love. Their response to our ministry was most gratifying, the greatest we had ever received anywhere. People walked forty and fifty miles to the meetings. Many wept when they met us, and their spiritual hunger and response to God made an impact upon our lives. God captured our hearts for these people, and as we left them we knew that someday God would bring us back.

The response on the part of Africans to our ministry has increased in subsequent years. In 1959 my family and I moved to Liberia, where we now have a home and headquarters at radio station ELWA; at present I am an Associate Evangelist on the Billy Graham Team. Our OPERATION AFRICA ministry consists of Gospel broadcasting, Christian literature, Christian films, and evangelistic crusades and Bible conferences. Each year we divide our time for crusade and Bible conference work between Africa, the United States, and other countries.

We conducted a Bible conference in Ethiopia, a conference sponsored by the Sudan Interior Mission. Every morning and evening it was my privilege to speak to crowds of from two to four thousand Ethiopian Christians.

One morning at one of the mission stations, the American Negro singer Jimmie McDonald and I were in our room preparing for the next meeting. We glanced out the window and there saw a great crowd of people staring at us. Taken by surprise, Jimmie asked: "Say, what's this? Why are these people standing outside our window?"

"Oh, it is all right, Jimmie," I replied. "Perhaps this is a little unusual for you since this is your first visit to Africa. But these people are just happy to see us. Most of them have never seen American Negroes, and this is their way of showing that we are welcome in their country."

We had a similar experience in Nairobi, Kenya. Jimmie McDonald, Bob Harrison, and I were walking down the street when three African young men approached us and said: "We are glad to have you American Negroes in our country." They left and told others. A great crowd gathered around us. A policeman drew near, thinking that a riot would break out, but such was not the case. These people were happy to know that we had come to minister to them in song and preaching the Word of God.

Later that same day at a Bible conference in the interior of Kenya, a few Christians after meeting us remarked: "Thank God for your coming. The prodigal sons have returned home."

These personal experiences confirm the fact that the Negro's ministry for Christ is generally accepted and greatly appreciated by people abroad. God's choice of a man or woman for Christian service is never based on color or race, but rather upon His sovereign grace and upon a person's willingness to respond to the call of God. Too long many white Christians have overlooked this truth. They act at times as though their white skin guarantees them a priority with God in Christian work. But God is not prejudiced in His dealings with the races of men. The Apostle Peter had to learn this lesson, he confessed: ". . . Of a truth I perceive that God is no respecter of persons: But in every nation he that feareth him, and worketh righteousness, is accepted with him" (ACTS 10:34,35).

The rise of nationalism in Africa and around the world creates a situation in which more Negro missionaries are needed on the mission fields today. While we are thankful for the few that are scattered here and there in different parts of the world, there is an increasing demand for more.

However, as we endeavor to secure additional Negroes for missionary work, there are certain problems we encounter. First, there are those problems which relate to white people themselves. For instance, we still meet the old problem of race prejudice in the attitude of some white missionaries toward Negroes. On the mission fields there are some white missionaries from various parts of the United States who are not able to hide their deep-seated racial prejudice against the black man. Naturally these missionaries are opposed to the idea of American Negroes serving as missionaries on the mission field.

This virus of racial prejudice is also projected in the lives of mission officials. One director of a missionary organization said: "Personally, I am in favor of using Negro missionaries on the mission field. But we have some men on our board who bitterly oppose the idea. My hands are tied because of those who, unfortunately, do not share my point of view."

Then there is the problem of a critical attitude on the part of white missionaries. There are missionaries on the field who question the African's ability to do first-class missionary work. This same attitude holds true in regard to work performed by American Negro missionaries. Many white missionaries still believe that if anything is going to be done and done properly, they must do it. They have a tendency to judge everything according to the standards that they themselves have set, and freely criticize the work of other races. Such an attitude makes it difficult at times for missionaries of color to work with them on the mission field.

Some white Christians today also fear that an increase of Negro missionaries on the field will result in interracial marriages. I have frankly discussed this problem with missionaries of both races and mission officials, both at home and abroad, and it is a very sensitive problem with many. Some use it as an excuse for not sending additional Negro missionaries to the fields.

I recall an experience with a few other Negro minister friends. We met with the foreign secretary of one of the large missionary organizations. We spoke to him about the need for his denomination using Negro missionaries on their stations in various parts of the world. After we presented our case, he said: "Yes, I know that our denomination should have Negro missionaries on our fields, but brethren, I do not believe in interracial marriages."

I must confess that his statement irritated me. I felt that he was using the problem of interracial marriage as a means of "passing the buck." Later I endeavored to assure him that I had not come to discuss interracial marriage on the mission field among missionaries, but rather to discuss the urgent matter of thrusting Negro missionaries out to the mission fields of the world, that these Christians might also have the opportunity to make their contributions for Jesus Christ.

Times are changing. Missionary organizations like the Sudan Interior Mission and others have dropped their "lily white" policies of racial discrimination against Negroes and are now ready to receive qualified Negroes as missionary candidates, but Negroes are not responding too well to invitations extended to them from their mission boards. This fact is frustrating to mission officials. One said: "I don't understand. Our organization has opened its doors now to Negroes. We want them to serve with our white missionaries on the fields. But where are the Negro young people? We have not been able to get a good response from them. We have had only a few applications, mostly from Negroes without the necessary qualifications. What can we do?"

"Well," I said, "for many years your organization had a policy not to accept Negroes. In the past there were qualified Negroes who applied but were turned down purely on the basis of their race and nothing else. Consequently, Negroes have not been favorably impressed with your testimony and work as a Christian organization."

I continued: "I am glad you have changed your policy and now stand ready to accept qualified Negroes as missionaries. But since you are not getting a good response from the Negro people you must not be discouraged. Remember, it is going to take time. You will have to exercise love and patience if you are to win Negroes to your program.

"Let me state further that the adoption of a mission policy to accept Negro missionary candidates is not sufficient. You must put your policy into action by devising an effective program of recruitment in regard to Negro missionary candidates. You must approach Negro ministers and outline your program. Inform these ministers and their congregations of your desire for Negro missionaries to serve with your mission.

"Seek opportunities for your missionaries to speak in Negro churches and present missionary films and slides of their work abroad. Let these missionaries strive to challenge Negro young men and women to dedicate their lives for missionary service.

"Another suggestion I would like to make is that you use your regular mission publications as a means to reach the Negro constituency with news about your mission and the need for Negro missionaries. If you are faithful in your efforts, in time results will come and there will be a gratifying response from the Negro people."

As one talks with Christians about the employment of Negro missionaries, the problem of finance always arises. As I have stated, more and more missionary organizations are scouting for Negro missionary candidates. But will these mission boards work faithfully and be just as sincere in raising money and other support for Negroes as they do for white missionaries? Will our many fine white evangelical churches continue to give liberally of their missionary money to faith missions and denominations if these organizations begin to recruit Negro missionaries for work on the mission fields?

Not only are there problems which face the white Christians in their quest for the Negro missionary, but there are problems which arise among the Negro people as well. There is the problem of getting more Negro people interested in missions. In the past, trying to interest more Negro young people in missions has been frustrating. For one thing, there were those who were really converted, loved the Lord, and wanted to work anywhere for Him in Christian service, but who lacked sufficient education and training for effective Christian work. On the other hand, there were Negro young men and women who possessed the necessary academic training and other qualifications, but were not real born-again Christians. But the picture is changing. It is possible now to find Negro young people who qualify both spiritually and academically—that is, there is a proper balance in their lives.

In recent years I have been greatly encouraged in visits to formerly all-white evangelical Bible schools, colleges, and seminaries to find a number of Negro students preparing themselves for full-time Christian service. There are Negroes who have graduated from the higher schools of learning and are seeking the Lord for His will in their lives as far as missions are concerned.

In Cleveland, Ohio, I talked with a young Negro doctor, an outstanding Christian. He said: "I am deeply interested in medical missionary work in Africa, and if the Lord directs, my wife and I are willing to go and do what we can to help our people on that continent."

In New York City a young Negro woman who had just finished her medical training spoke with me about the great need for doctors on the mission field. She said: "I am praying and looking to the Lord for His will for my life. I know about the wonderful opportunities for service for Christ on the mission field."

A Negro teacher in the New York public school system remarked: "I feel that the Lord is leading me to be a missionary teacher in Africa."

These are just a few of the testimonies one hears today from Christian Negro young men and women. God is moving upon their hearts, and more and more of them feel the call of God for Christian missions. It is incumbent upon us, therefore, that we pray that the Spirit of God may soon thrust them out to the regions beyond.

It is also a fact that a large percentage of our Christian young people today are suspicious of the kind overtures that are coming to them from white Christians. These young people are aware of the change of policy that some white missionary organizations have made in regard to Negro missionaries, and they are happy about the change. However, in my conversations with them I have been challenged with this question: "Well, Howard, do you really believe that these white people are sincere? You know that for years they have closed the door in our faces because of our race, and now they are beginning to invite us to join their organizations and serve with them. Do they now mean business, or are they just fooling around?"

In this current trend toward total integration in America, I sincerely believe that the Negro people need, whenever the occasion and opportunity arises, to work together with people of all races in the work of evangelism and missions. An integrated team of Christians, working harmoniously together for the evangelization of the whole world for the glory of God, is the greatest demonstration of the love and the saving grace of God in our hearts as Christians. Such a demonstration proves to the world that in Jesus Christ there is no racial difference or discrimination. And who can withstand such?

Another problem is: will Negro missionaries receive adequate financial support from Negro churches? Many Negro young people today would launch out in a missionary ministry abroad if they honestly felt that their churches would faithfully stand behind them. Instead these young people are discouraged by the fact that many wealthy and prospering Negro churches are without a vision for missions and fail to fulfill their financial responsibility to support missionaries. It is equally disheartening when they see the poorer congregations that are not able to sufficiently support their ministers and the work of the church; these ministers are often forced to take secular work to supplement their meager church income. What encouragement is there for Negro young people when this situation exists? If we expect to see an increase of Negro missionaries on the foreign fields, the Negro churches in America must awake to their own financial obligations to their missionaries.

We have cited some of the most pressing problems which both Negro and white Christians face today as they consider the Negro missionary and his ministry. I fully realize that there are other problems. But it is my firm conviction that we can no longer afford to evade these or any obstacles that may arise. The time has come when both Negroes and whites must face them and take the necessary steps to solve them. It is evident that the Negro does have an important ministry for Christ on the mission fields today, and when given an equal opportunity will prove by the help of God that his ministry is just as effective as that of the whites.

White Christians must understand the supreme worth of the Negro missionary in this day and time. In the Inter-Varsity book, *Missions in Crisis,* the authors (Eric S. Fife and Arthur F. Glasser) convey this thought: "In the years ahead, if we still have years in which to accomplish our task, the Church must rapidly mobilize her full resources. This will certainly include the non-Caucasian—unless we permit our race prejudice, and our poverty of imagination and faith, to kill his potential contribution. It may well be that, when the history of the Church is finally written, the next decade may be called the day of the non-Caucasian."

This is the golden hour for Negroes to awake to their responsibility to worldwide evangelism and missions. Some are preparing themselves for overseas service with the Peace Corps, and this is good. But where are those who will enlist in God's missionary corps and carry the Gospel to the ends of the earth? Missionary organizations are calling for Negroes to minister on the mission fields of the world as evangelists, teachers, Bible translators, directors of youth centers, journalists, Christian book salesmen, printers, artists, doctors, nurses, radio technicians, and pilots. To answer this call it is necessary for Negro young men and women to prepare themselves.

Dr. A. B. Simpson, that great missionary leader, once said: "We want men and women who are thoroughly converted and know it. We want men and women who are fully consecrated to God, sanctified by the blood of Jesus Christ and filled with the Holy Spirit so saved from themselves that they are at leisure to work for others.

"We want men and women who are burning with the love of souls and are longing to lead men and women to Christ. We want men and women who know the Lord so well that they can have His joy under all circumstances, who will not be afraid of loneliness nor privation; who ask no greater recompense than the privilege of serving and pleasing Him, and who go out not wanting sympathy, but rejoicing in the name of missionary, and the privilege of enduring suffering and even shame for the name of Him who died for them.

"We want men and women who have such a distinct call to the mission field that they cannot stay back, and even if we do not send them they will go somehow.

"May the Lord send us a thousand such men."

7

Racism and Missions

HAS DISCRIMINATION AGAINST Negroes in America had any effect on the missionary enterprise in Africa?

Yes, Africa and other countries throughout the world are acutely aware of the serious racial problem in the United States. The best and worst of our American way of life are projected abroad. But the projection of America's sins gets the greater coverage and publicity, especially the sin of discrimination.

Too many Americans are unaware of this. We seem to think that our daily life and conduct are shrouded in secrecy and unknown to the outside world. Such is not the case. Instead, every aspect of our living in America, whether good or bad, is open before the world for inspection, examination, and criticism.

This was forcefully impressed upon me in 1957 when my wife and I made our first visit to Africa. I conducted evangelistic crusades in Liberia, Ghana, and Nigeria, and the response to the Gospel was most gratifying. Our personal contacts with Africans from all walks of life revealed their deep spiritual hunger for God and the Bible. We observed that Africans have a keen and sincere interest in the social and racial problems of America.

From the modern cities to the underdeveloped bush sections of the country, Africans plagued us with questions concerning Dr. Martin Luther King and the 1955 bus boycott in Montgomery, Alabama. They quizzed us about the Emmett Till lynching in Mississippi and other racial disturbances. I was amazed at the vast amount of factual information possessed by African people on the problem of racism and discrimination in America. Deeply curious, I inquired as to the source of their information.

One African remarked, "Oh, we read *Time* and *Newsweek* and our own daily newspapers."

Another said, "We keep informed by listening to our short-wave radios. We hear the world news each day over Voice of America, the BBC, and Radio Moscow."

Still another commented, "I know all about America's race problem. I was confronted with it as a student during my stay in the States."

Admittedly, the African people are better informed today on America's discriminatory practices than they were seven years ago when I made my first trip to Africa. More and more Africans are coming to the United States for education, with 6,100 in our colleges and universities at present. Many Africans are also here as official representatives of their countries.

In Africa the number of radios, newspapers, magazines, and books is great. In a few countries television provides entertainment and up-to-the-minute news reports. Consequently, Africa keeps well abreast with the news of America's racial flare-ups in Alabama, Georgia, Mississippi, New York, New Jersey, Philadelphia, Chicago, Los Angeles, and elsewhere.

Since 1959 I have been spending a good part of my time in Liberia, West Africa, with my family. As a result of many trips across the continent for evangelistic crusades and Bible conferences, I know that the problem of racism in America continues to hurt and hinder the work of Christian missions in Africa. It has the following particularly damaging results.

It effects government leaders. Many of the powerful African leaders of the independent nations in Africa today are actually products of Christian missions. These men received their early religious training and education from the missionaries and mission schools. Fortunately, a few have expressed their faith in Jesus Christ, in the Bible, and in Christianity. They are now outstanding Christian witnesses.

However, their Christian faith is sorely tested when they come to the United States. In America Africans are also exposed to racism and discrimination. Because of the color of their skin, they are frequently mistreated and mocked. They suffer abusive words and threats from white racists. Africans have found that they cannot eat in some restaurants. They have not been given the right to rent or buy homes in the white neighborhoods. Some colleges and universities have refused to admit them. Even when they are finally accepted in schools, in far too many cases their lives are plagued by loneliness—the tormenting loneliness that comes to a Negro when he is not fully accepted and respected in the white man's society.

In America, Africans often become frustrated, discouraged, and disillusioned. They cannot reconcile Christ, Christianity, and the Bible with racial prejudice and segregation. As one young African said recently at an international church conference in Switzerland: "Africans cannot understand how white Americans can claim to be practicing Christians and, at the same time, deny human rights to fellow American Christians who are colored."

It is understandable, then, why some Africans return to their countries with misgivings about America and her missionary program abroad. Eventually some government leaders lose interest in Christian missions. Others become bitter and antagonistic toward all white missionaries and the Christian church in Africa. A few Christian Africans unfortunately experience complete shipwreck of their Christian faith.

On this point it would be only fair to say that in spite of all the criticism which is being leveled against missionaries due to America's racial problem, a few government leaders still champion the ministry of Christian missions in Africa. An example is the president of Liberia, Dr. William V. S.

Tubman, who not only has distinguished himself as one of the outstanding leaders in Africa, but is a churchman and a friend to missionaries.

Our racial problem in America effects missionaries themselves. A great deal of embarrassment, shame, and guilt come to them. For instance, an African will ask a missionary the question: "What state do you come from in the United States?" Such a question today does not provoke an enjoyable or pleasant conversation between the African and the missionary. For this reason many missionaries are ashamed and rather reluctant to admit that they are from certain states where serious racial incidents often occur.

As a Negro I work and have fellowship with white missionaries from Europe, Australia, and America. Frequently our conversations turn to the race problem. They say that something must be done immediately to solve the problem in America because of its damaging effects upon the work of the Lord in Africa and other parts of the world.

Strangely enough I have discovered that many American missionaries have never had any contacts with American Negroes before coming to Africa. On one occasion my wife and I were guests in the home of an American missionary couple in Nigeria, West Africa. During our conversation at the supper table, the hostess made this observation: "This is the first time we have ever had American Negroes in our home. Isn't it strange that our Christian fellowship together can be in Africa but not in the United States?"

She continued: "We know and we are ashamed to say that you would not be welcomed in our home or even in our church in the South. This whole racial problem is inconsistent with our Christian witness."

Then, too, frustration and despair often haunt the lives of missionaries. They labor faithfully for the Gospel. They expose themselves to all kinds of disease and danger to liberate the African people from sin, sickness, and ignorance. Yet many Africans do not trust the missionaries because they are part of "white America" living in Africa, the black man's continent. In short, the spirit of black nationalism in Africa today causes missionaries to be aware that their white skin is more of a liability than a help in their efforts to evangelize the African with the Gospel of Christ.

In view of the fierce winds of change which sweep across Africa, it is desperately necessary that we pray for our missionaries. Their task is a most difficult one in the new Africa. Missionaries have done and are doing a tremendous job to complete the unfinished task of evangelism and missions there. But their necessary ministries for Christ are hindered and their position jeopardized because of the problem of racism in America. Through love, kindness, and sincerity many missionaries have won the respect of the African people. Other missionaries have not been so successful.

Discrimination against Negroes in America has a serious effect on the followers of non-Christian religions and African extremists. The Muslims use the racial problem in America to advance their cause in Africa. Muslims preach and teach that Christianity is a white man's religion, that Jesus Christ is the white man's Saviour, that the Bible is the white man's Bible. Muslims contend that Christianity offers no valid salvation or redemption for the black man. Using the race issue to prove that Christianity is inferior to Islam, Muslims continue to make great progress in their untiring efforts to win Africa.

Communists also take full advantage of America's racial problem for their own purpose in Africa. Currently Russians and Red Chinese are competing to conquer and control the continent. Communists capitalize on the unrest, strife, turmoil, and chaos among the African people to promote their own ideology.

Many times in our home in Liberia I have listened on a shortwave set to the powerful transmissions of Radio Moscow and Radio Peking. Programs in English and in many of the African languages are offered. I listened as the announcers told how Negroes were being treated in America, how dogs and fire hoses were turned on them. I heard about Negro churches and homes being bombed and burned by the segregationists. This news saddened me. I knew that my feelings were shared by my African and missionary colleagues. We knew that the broadcasting of such tragic news by the Communists defaces America's image abroad, and impedes the progress of Christian missions in Africa, Asia, and other parts of the world.

At times the racial problem we face in America seems hopeless. However, "with God all things are possible." Certainly there are some things we can now do to improve the situation, and remove some of the damaging effects.

America will have to be more militant in her fight to remove racism and discrimination from this country, and speedily grant first-class citizenship and equal rights to all Negro Americans. So long as Jim Crowism remains, this country cannot hope to command respect and honor from other nations.

All racism must be erased from our schools, colleges, and universities. A few schools, including Christian institutions, have a policy that prohibits the acceptance of American Negroes or anyone else of the Negro race.

Recently an African young man, a product of Christian missions in East Africa, came to America on government business. Before leaving his country, he expressed a desire to study theology in some Christian school in the United States. A white missionary recommended a certain outstanding school in the South. Upon his arrival in this country the young man applied to the school, but was quickly rejected. In a letter from the school registrar, the African was informed that the school had a policy not to accept anyone with "black blood." The African is now discouraged and embittered due to his confrontation with racism in America, the homeland of white missionaries who traveled to Africa to tell his people about the love of Jesus Christ, the Saviour. The young man is now a delegate to the United Nations, and unless he allows God to help him overcome this unfortunate experience he could become lost to the cause of Christ.

All discriminatory policies and practices against Negroes must be abolished by white missionary societies in this country. For years many qualified Negro young men and women have felt the call of God for service on the mission field. They applied to mission boards, but were not accepted because of their race. This evil practice has caused many Negro young people to lose confidence in the testimony of white Christians. It has also hurt the cause of Christian missions, as if interpreting to the colored people of the world that The Great Commission of Jesus Christ was given exclusively to the Caucasian race.

My conversations with mission officials of various denominations reveal that some missionary organizations have had the vision and courage to change their policies. However, a few missionary societies still refuse to recruit Negroes for their program. This is tragic indeed. We should earnestly pray that these missionary organizations will abolish their non-Scriptural and dishonorable policy of racial discrimination and take immediate steps to integrate their mission family. The sooner the better.

In light of the Negro revolution in America and the black nationalism currently sweeping Africa, mission officials in this country should screen their missionary candidates more carefully than in the past. Aside from the spiritual, academic, and physical qualifications required, missionary recruits must be examined about their attitudes on the race question. Do they have any racial prejudice? Are they possessed with the feeling of white superiority?

A few missionaries in Africa have become unpopular and unacceptable. Why? Because they project the wrong attitudes toward the African people. For this reason all new missionaries must experience a mighty baptism of the love and compassion of Christ before they leave for service abroad. The love of Christ will enable them to labor among the African people, not as masters but as humble servants of God, who sincerely believe that the key to the unfinished task of evangelism in Africa today is not the foreign missionary, but rather the African himself.

Recently, the *New York Times* presented a few statements of Rev. C. E. Autrey, evangelism director of the Southern Baptist Mission Board. The *Times* quoted Mr. Autrey as saying: "You cannot love and hate with the same heart, and today we are trying to generate a church without the basic ingredient of the New Testament—love for people. Our attitude towards people of other races is definitely curbing our evangelistic outreach, both at home and around the world."

What action will the church take? Time is running out on us. "For the time is come that judgment must begin at the house of God . . ." (PETER 4:17).

8

The Race Problem—
A Challenge to the Christian Church

THE MIRROR OF modern race relations reflects the Christian church in America as ashamed and guilty before God and society. Weighed in the balances of divine justice it is found wanting. Such a picture of the church is pathetic but realistic.

Kyle Haselden, in *The Racial Problem in Christian Perspective,* says: "This is the story of the white Christian people and their churches in relationship to the Negroes of America. So far as the major denominations are concerned, it is the story of indifference, vacillation, and duplicity, with occasional interludes in which the church came alive to its duty only to sink after a time into renewed indifference. It is a history in which the church not only compromised its ethic to the mood and practice of the times but was itself actively unethical, sanctioning the enslavement of human beings, producing the patterns of segregation, urging upon the oppressed Negro the extracted sedatives of the Gospel, and promulgating a doctrine of interracial morality which is itself immoral. It is a story in which many of the errors and deliberate evils of the past are firmly entrenched in the present and give warning of their intention to move with us into the future."

Too long has the church been silent and miserably weak on the race issue. The church has failed to speak out against racism and the other social injustices of our day. Had the church taken a bold, uncompromising stand against the plague of racial segregation and discrimination in the past, America would not be confronted with the disgraceful problem of racism she has in the present. The church has not provided the necessary spiritual leadership and moral integrity to America in the area of race relations. Indeed, many churches help champion the cause of Jim Crowism and racial bigotry by their silence or neutrality.

Admittedly the church is making some progress in this field. Not long ago I visited one of the outstanding white evangelical churches in the country. In the past this church was opposed to integration. While a few Negroes attended services, they could not become members. But now the situation has completely changed. Under the pastor's Bible-centered and Spirit-filled preaching and ministry of love to all people, Negroes increasingly attend, finding in the church a constant source of spiritual blessing and help. The choir is integrated. There were at least 70 Negro worshippers in a congregation of 900 or more. At the close of the service the minister extended the right hand of fellowship to new members, one of whom was a Negro woman.

Occasionally a Negro church embraces white people in its membership, and in some cases white ministers are pastors of Negro churches and vice versa. Negro and white ministers meet together in denominational and interdenominational church and community projects. Negro and white bishops and moderators are appointed to serve both races in their denominations.

In the field of evangelism, Billy Graham conducts integrated crusades around the world. His ministry continues to make a tremendous spiritual impact upon the Christian church and the nation, and incidentally improves relations between the races.

Christian organizations such as the American and the New York Bible Societies and others have for years had Negroes on their staffs. More recently various other Christian organizations have employed Negroes.

Recently when I was speaking at a white Bible conference and youth camp in New England, a gifted Negro couple was serving as an evangelistic team, and they assumed other administrative duties as staff members. A most significant step was the election in 1965 of Dr. William R. Tolbert, vice-president of Liberia, as the first Negro president of the Baptist World Alliance.

But despite such evidence of progress, the church is still far behind in the crusade against racism. The church continues to drag its feet and hesitates to come to grips with the problem. Having slept through a revolution in this country, the church now awakens to find herself spiritually incapable of casting out the demon of racial prejudice. Consequently the Sunday morning worship service in most churches is still America's most segregated hour. This fact can be illustrated by a recent incident in Americus, Georgia. A group of Negroes, trying to enter one of the white churches, were stopped on the steps by a member, who said: "We don't have room for you."

In this matter I sincerely believe that the white evangelical and fundamental churches need a strong rebuke. Devoting themselves to the preaching of the Gospel, they have evaded the racial problem. Regarding the race issue as purely social, they have left it for society to handle. Proud of their allegiance to the Gospel, for years they have chided the liberals for their departure from the faith. Now they find themselves in an embarrassing position, as the liberal ministers point an accusing finger at them for not becoming sufficiently involved in the crusade. Many Gospel preachers are in general opposed to the freedom-march demonstrations and civil-rights movement. Within their camp are outright segregationists, in pulpit and pew. They deride the Supreme Court decision of May 17, 1954, and proclaim the civil-rights movement to be communist-inspired and energized by the devil. Many liberals show far more love and concern for the Negro and his struggles. They champion the cause of civil rights, and seek by deliberate action to destroy the cancer of racism within church and nation.

Parodoxically, many white evangelicals who confess their

love for Jesus Christ, believe the Bible to be the infallible and authoritative Word of God, preach a separated, Spirit-filled life, and stand for the pure doctrines of our historic Christian faith, are yet actually insincere at heart because they demonstrate no love or interest in the spiritual and social welfare of the American Negro. They have no vision to help evangelize our unsaved and unchurched masses. Normal procedure is for them to panic and quickly place their churches or homes up for sale and leave the moment the first Negro family moves into the neighborhood. Yet these same Christians pride themselves on their ability to raise thousands of dollars annually in their church missionary conventions to send white missionaries to Africa to evangelize the black man on that continent. Such hypocrisy brings a reproach on the work of God and wounds the loving and compassionate heart of our Lord, who sacrificed His precious life on the cross for the redemption of all people, regardless of race or color.

One wonders how they can honestly contend for the Christian faith and preach the whole counsel of God without dealing with the problem of discrimination and segregation in the church. In this crisis hour, how can these Christians remain insensitive to their social, moral, and spiritual obligation to the Negro? The Bible unquestionably is the greatest book on justice in the world, yet these Christians, preaching the Bible, evade the race issue and close their eyes to the terrible social injustices imposed upon the Negro in this country. White evangelicals must explain before God and society how they can reconcile their love for Christ and loyalty to the Bible with race prejudice and bigotry.

It is not easy for a Negro to worship in some white churches, even though permitted to do so. When he attends the services he is often confronted with the popular "white stare," as though he were some strange creature from outer space. If he takes a seat next to a white person, that person may find a quick excuse to find a seat elsewhere. And if there is an empty seat next to a Negro, it is likely to be one of the last to be occupied by the white people who arrive subsequently.

During the service the Negro worshipper often experiences a haunting loneliness and a sense of estrangement. The preacher speaks on the subject of "Our Oneness in Christ as Believers," but the Negro knows that there are few white Christians who really practice this truth in their daily associations with Negroes. Such a worshipper is aware that his dark skin is a barrier which keeps many white Christians from respecting him as a true brother in the Lord.

At the conclusion of the church service the Negro worshipper may be greeted by a few smiles from the minister and parishioners and the usual remark: "We are happy to have you in our church this morning. Please come again." But he knows from experience that such actions do not necessarily mean that he was really welcome or that the people meant what they said. Negroes know that many whites (like sinners of every hue) have a knack for saying one thing but meaning something else. The Negro realizes that if he returns to the same church the next Sunday, some of the previously polite people may completely ignore him so as to remind him of his "place."

Once while attending a Bible conference in an eastern city I listened attentively as one of the featured speakers preached on "The Indwelling Christ" and was blessed with the message. At one point in the sermon, however, I was shocked when the preacher began to tell a story about a "nigger." His joke brought a tremendous amount of laughter from the white audience. Then with embarrassment he recognized me in the congregation, stopped preaching, and said: "Brother, I want you to know that I did not mean to speak deprecatingly of your race. I told that joke to illustrate a point in my sermon. Please forgive me."

After his message many people went forward to the altar, I with them. I prayed that God would forgive this man, cleanse his heart of prejudice, and fill him with the love of God. I also asked that God would give me the grace to remain throughout the rest of the conference and to keep the love of Christ in my own heart.

Several years ago while conducting a radio ministry in New York City I received a letter from a Christian white woman. She wrote that she and her family enjoyed our church choir and the message from the Word of God. She included a check for the support of our broadcast. As time progressed this woman became a regular listener and supporter of our ministry. One day she called me on the telephone and said: "Reverend Jones, we have enjoyed your broadcasts so much that we want to invite you to our home. We call you our 'radio pastor.' We desire that you come and have prayer with our family. Will you accept our invitation?"

"Yes, I will be happy to come," I replied. "And if it is all right with you, I will plan to call next Sunday afternoon."

From her many letters and gifts I knew she was wealthy and lived in one of the exclusive sections of Long Island. I wondered just how she would react when I made my visit to her home.

Sunday came and I drove out to Long Island with my little daughter. We located the house, and I rang the bell. The door opened, and an elderly woman came to the door.

"Good afternoon, my name is Reverend Jones."

The woman looked at me for a moment and said: "Oh, Reverend Jones, please come in. We have been expecting you."

My daughter and I entered the house, and before we were seated a door opened from a nearby room. A young woman came out, took one look at me, and stepped quickly back into the room and slammed the door. Immediately a loud argument took place, but we were unable to detect the meaning.

Embarrassed, the elderly woman said: "I am indeed sorry for what is happening. That was my daughter who just came out. I must tell you that none of us knew you were a Negro. My daughter, especially, is quite outspoken in her dislike for the colored people. Please forgive us."

We were then invited to be seated. Eventually another daughter came into the front room and greeted us. She asked

124

my daughter if she would like a glass of milk and a piece of cake. My daughter accepted her offer, and the two withdrew into the kitchen. Turning to me the woman said: "Your radio ministry has been a great source of spiritual blessing to me, and I am glad we have been able to help support your work. However, I must say that we are really surprised to discover that you are a Negro."

"Why?" I asked.

"Because you don't sound like one on the radio," she replied.

"Well, the fact that I am a Negro ought not to make any difference, should it? God made me what I am, and I am not ashamed of it," I said.

"You are right," she said. "You are giving out the Word of God, and your ministry is helping people."

We continued to talk about spiritual matters, but I could see she was disturbed about my racial identity. Finally I mentioned it was time for us to go. We bowed our heads, had a moment of prayer together, and then shook hands, and my daughter and I left. I never heard from her again.

There was the instance of another white radio listener of ours, a woman who was an outstanding poet in New York. She listened to our broadcast each Sunday and sent us contributions. This contact ceased when she discovered we were Negroes. We had sent her a newsletter which had pictures of our radio staff.

In the days of my pastorate in New York some of our white radio listeners would drive to our church, walk in, then quickly depart after discovering it was a Negro church.

Recently a white minister told me that a wealthy white woman decided to leave a handsome legacy to his church. The only condition was that the church would promise never to allow Negroes in its membership. Two white families left that church after the pastor had dedicated a Negro baby one Sunday morning.

Then there is the case of another white church that voted to integrate its membership. Thirty white families, some of the best financial supporters in the church, walked out. Consequently, missionary giving decreased. One man who had been supporting a missionary couple in Africa said to the pastor: "I am not in favor of integration; therefore I will have to leave the church."

"But what about your support toward our missionaries on the field?" inquired the pastor.

"I am sorry," replied the man, "but that will also be stopped. I'm going to take my money somewhere else."

These cases indicate how insincere some white Christians are in regard to Negroes. Their practices are contrary to the Word of God. These Christians have obviously forgotten that Jesus preached against hypocrisy in the hearts of the religious people of His day. Christ said: "Woe unto you, scribes and Pharisees, hypocrites! for ye make clean the outside of the cup and of the platter, but within they are full of extortion and excess. Thou blind Pharisee, cleanse first that which is within the cup and platter, that the outside of them may be clean also. Woe unto you, scribes and Pharisees, hypocrites! for ye are like unto whited sepulchres, which indeed appear beautiful outward, but are within full of dead men's bones, and of all uncleanness. Even so ye also outwardly appear righteous unto men, but within ye are full of hypocrisy and iniquity" (MATTHEW 23:25-28).

It is the will of God that Christians should be sincere in their relation to Him and their fellowmen. The Apostle Paul emphasized this truth in speaking to the believers in the church at Philippi: "That ye may approve things that are excellent; that ye may be sincere and without offence till the day of Christ" (PHILIPPIANS 1:10).

It is encouraging in these days of racial tension and conflict to meet white Christians who are sincere and genuine, those who love all people regardless of race or color. These Christians are deeply concerned about the situation we face, and are in full sympathy with the Negro and the problems which

126

confront him in America. These white friends of the Negro oppose all forms of racial segregation and discrimination, and not only talk about brotherly love but demonstrate it in many ways in helping to erase the color barrier in the American church and society. They welcome the opportunity to discuss the race problem in frankness and with an open mind so as to seek a better understanding between the races.

In my travels as an evangelist I am frequently asked what it is like to be a member of the Billy Graham Team. In answer to that question I inform people that for more than eight years my being on the Team has been one continuous spiritual blessing and challenge in my own heart and life and ministry. One finds that love prevails on the Team for Jesus Christ, the Word of God, and souls of men. There is a spirit of loyalty on the part of the Team for its leader, Billy Graham. Many times I have thanked God for these dedicated men who are solely committed to one supreme task: the evangelization of the whole world with the Gospel of Jesus Christ, in the power of the Holy Spirit, and by the use of radio, T.V., films, literature, and other facilities.

During the early years of my association with the Graham Team in mass crusades I was confronted with certain problems which required personal adjustments on my part in dealing with all races. I found I had to prepare myself spiritually so that I might represent Christ and the Team in a way pleasing to God. Especially was this true in the area of race relations.

At the invitation of Billy Graham I joined the Team in 1957 to work in the New York Crusade. The fact that I was the first Negro Team member made news across the country. Immediately I was conscious of the fact that many whites who attended the crusade resented my being with the organization, and their looks and actions convinced me that they were prejudiced. Now, as I look back, certain incidents come to mind.

One day a white crusade committee member phoned a Negro minister in the city, not knowing that the Negro clergyman was a personal friend of mine. In the conversation the committeeman acknowledged his curiosity about me, and asked: "Would you mind telling me how Howard Jones got on the Billy Graham Team?"

Another time a large reception was given in honor of Billy and the Team by a prominent member of the local crusade committee. At the reception I was the only Negro present. I felt quite uncomfortable at times because a few of the people glared at me. Loneliness gnawed at me, and I felt estranged in the midst of a group of people, most of whom I did not know. Some were very friendly towards me, but others were cool and indifferent. I must confess that I kept wishing the reception would end, and this wish was intensified when I overheard the conversation of two white ministers. One said: "How did he get here?"

On another occasion I recall a conversation with Billy. He was deeply concerned about a problem relative to the crusade and said: "Howard, we praise God for the way He is blessing in this crusade. Thousands are attending each night and hundreds continue to make decisions for Christ. However, I am rather disturbed because I feel that more Negroes ought to attend. Here in New York there are thousands of them, and I want the Negro people to know that these crusades are not just for the white people, but for all people. Do you have any suggestions as to how we might get more Negro people to attend the crusade?"

"Billy," I said, "I believe that if you would personally visit Harlem and conduct a meeting there, this would establish a point of contact with the Negro community. And I sincerely believe we would have a good meeting."

"But do you think they would consider my visit to Harlem as being a segregated move on our part?"

"No, I don't. By going to Harlem you would be extending your ministry to the Negro people there. The people, I'm sure, will appreciate your coming, and you will win many friends, who in turn will come to the crusade at the Garden."

"All right," Billy replied, "I will go to Harlem. Let us pray that God may bless our ministry in reaching many people for Jesus Christ."

News of our proposed Harlem visit was released to the press. Soon the crusade office received phone calls and letters from people who showed a great interest in the meeting. A few of the letters revealed how race prejudice motivated people to say some very unkind things to Billy. One white man wrote: "Billy, now you are going to ruin your whole ministry by going up there to Harlem to preach to the 'niggers'."

But the fact is that our visit to Harlem did not ruin the ministry of the Graham Team, but rather was a blessing to us all. Thousands of Negroes and many whites turned out to see and hear the evangelist. Music was furnished by two outstanding Negro choirs and George Beverly Shea. Billy preached the Word of God, and many responded to the call of Christ. The Sunday afternoon outdoor meeting was covered by the press, radio, and TV. All agreed that a spiritual impact had been made upon Harlem, and as a result of that meeting and another similar one held the following Sunday afternoon in Brooklyn, Negro attendance and participation in the New York Crusade noticeably increased.

It was during the New York Crusade that Miss Ethel Waters rededicated her life to Jesus Christ. She sang in the crusade choir for sixteen of the seventeen weeks. Her solos in the Garden and on the crusade television programs brought real blessing to thousands, and it was clearly evident that her presence and participation in the meetings helped to win more Negroes and even whites to the crusades.

Many times I know that Billy Graham has been acutely conscious of the problems I would face as a Negro in dealing with those whites who were antagonistic to me because of my race and were not too happy about my being on the Team. However, Billy's humble and Christ-like spirit created an atmosphere of love around his Team which made it quite uncomfortable for those with race prejudice to do anything that would destroy the bond of unity which holds us together.

129

There have been occasions at receptions when Billy would introduce me first, before other Team members, just to establish the fact that I was as much part of his Team as anyone else. In all my years with the Team there has never been any paternalistic spirit exhibited by Billy on my behalf, nor have I received any preferential treatment from him just because I was the first Negro with the association. My ministry with the Team has been a spiritual fellowship with those who love the Lord and each other. Therefore when people ask me if Billy Graham is really sincere in his attitude towards Negroes, I am compelled to say "yes," on the basis of my personal associations with him. I have had opportunities to observe him in many situations when it would have been easier for him to be silent on the race issue so as to win friends and influence people. But his positive stand against racism in the Christian church and in the nation, his recent action in adding two more Negroes to his Team, Rev. Ralph Bell, Associate Evangelist, and Jimmie McDonald, soloist, and his willingness to do whatever possible to bring about a better understanding between whites and Negroes by the Christian approach have caused him to suffer the loss of friends and financial support.

He comments on this in his book, *World Aflame:* "I believe that Christians must take a stand on the moral, social, and spiritual issues of our day. I had not been preaching long before I decided that I would never preach to another segregated audience in any situation over which we had control. This was long before the Supreme Court decision of 1954. I lost many supporters. I received many threatening letters. I was called a communist. Certain churches no longer would have me in their pulpits. However, I felt this was the Christian position and I could do no other."

In this crusade against racism in the church other sincere white ministers have been involved in one way or another. In recent months two white ministers and a seminary student have been killed and two other ministers injured. White ministers have lost their churches, had crosses burned on their lawns, and experienced threats and persecutions at the hands of racists because of their stand against segregation and discrimination. These clergymen are often called "nigger lovers" by their loved ones and friends. We admire the courage of these men who will not keep silent on the race issue and who are dedicated to the cause of destroying the last bit of racism in the church and nation. Would to God that we had more such sincere white ministers. The fact that there are so few is appalling. This duplicity of action, insincerity of spirit, and lack of love among so many white Christians baffle Negroes and cause them to doubt the validity of the white man's Christianity.

There are white Christians who argue that the Negro is inferior because of his color and position in life. They feel that the Negro is foreordained to suffer because he is under the "curse of Ham," that God consigned him forever to a place of servitude.

One white woman expressed such a view in a letter to Billy Graham after viewing one of his telecasts. "We heard your television plea for love for the colored people. Most people understand that love has its limitation according to circumstances and needs. What does the colored race really need? Have you ever heard that the Negro is a seminoid—that is, half human and half spirit? That Negroes are in a state of reincarnation, charred from the fires of hell, working their way back to life individually, by degree, some becoming good Christians, and many, many still in the lusts, the hates, and the deceptions that charred them?

"Did you know that every colored man, woman, and child is a mentalist (mind reader and voodooist)? That they can and are seeping their spirits into the whites whom they get a 'key' on (by an object, letter, or impression from the mind even of another?) Do you realize why they want at least one of their kind in every school, neighborhood, and organization everywhere? Do you think God requires that his Christian people submit to this? Do you think He inspires some public speakers to shame the white for resisting?"

When my son was in kindergarten he was once confronted with this problem. Upon returning home he said: "Mother, what is wrong with my color?"

"Nothing is wrong with your color, David. Why do you ask?" replied his mother.

"Because today in school a little white girl told me that I had the wrong color because I was not white."

When I came home I took my son aside and assured him that nothing was wrong with his color, because God made it that way; that three-fourths of the world population is colored.

Dr. Rufus Jones tells of a boy who was standing with his father at a country fair. A man was releasing small balloons of various colors—some red, others blue, and others white. "Dad," inquired the lad, observing their flight, "Why did that red balloon fly higher than the others?"

The wise father replied, "Son, it's not the color that counts, but what's inside."

Upon what Scriptural grounds is the argument of Negro inferiority based? A favorite citation is from the book of Genesis. You might recall the embarrassing scene. Noah, evidently unaware of the potency of fermented grape juice, had been overcome. As he lay "uncovered within his tent," his sons came upon him. Ham, the father of Canaan, made the discovery and reported the matter to his two brothers, Shem and Japheth, who took a garment and covered their father, while modestly looking in the opposite direction so that "they saw not their father's nakedness." We read, "And Noah awoke from his wine, and knew what his younger son had done unto him. And he said, Cursed be Canaan; a servant of servants shall he be unto his brethren. And he said, Blessed be the Lord God of Shem; and Canaan shall be his servant" (GENESIS 9:20-27).

But is this actually a proof-text? Or do those who use it

132

thereby reveal that they are "unlearned and unstable wrest, as they do also the other scriptures, unto their own destruction" (II PETER 3:16)?

A true Biblical interpretation and understanding of this matter is needed. Dr. Clyde T. Francisco, professor of Old Testament at Southern Baptist Theological Seminary, Louisville, Kentucky, says: "This passage in no way relates to the present tensions between the races; when made to do so it has been misinterpreted and misapplied. It makes no reference to the Negro in any way. Whatever the reason, the curse of servitude was on Canaan, not Ham, and the modern Negro is not one of Canaan's descendants. The use of the passage to foster racial superiority is an obvious attempt to prove by the Bible a position previously held for quite different reasons. The Bible should be studied in order to correct our attitudes and judge our prejudice, not to reconfirm our previous misconceptions.

"Genesis 9:18–19 proclaims that all men are descended from Noah and thus have the same common ancestor. If all men belong to the same family, they should be able to live together in that one family in peace. . . ."

In God's sight there is no such thing as white, black, red, brown, or yellow superiority. God lays all men low in the dust when He tells them that: "All have sinned and come short of the glory of God." All races were created in the image of God and came into the world through our first parents, Adam and Eve. Because of man's sin and rebellion against God, He sent His Son into the world to become the Saviour of all mankind. Though He was sinless, He became sin by taking upon Himself the sins of the Negro, the white man, and all other races of men. Christ was made a curse for us because all men were under the curse and judgment of sin. But the Bible says that: "Christ hath redeemed us from the curse of the law, being made a curse for us: for it is written, Cursed is everyone that hangest on a tree" (GALATIANS 3:13).

The Bible clearly establishes the fact that the only real curse

133

imposed upon all men is that of sin, a curse which Christ removed by His sacrificial death on the cross. The argument that the Negro is inferior because of the curse of Ham is a spurious, fallacious one. Too long has the Bible been used by men to buttress their positions.

Prior to the Civil War the white masters often conducted religious services for their slaves. It was a practice of white preachers to select a text from the book of Philemon or other Epistles of Paul. A favorite text was: "Slaves, be obedient to them that are your masters . . . as unto Christ." When some of the slaves learned to read, they assiduously avoided Paul's letters, because they felt that he had consigned them to interminable slavery. Had not the preachers told that if they remained good and obedient slaves, God would bless them?

J. A. Rogers, a noted Negro historian, comments: "To make sure that the blacks would remain inferior the masters made it a crime to teach a slave to read. He could have the Bible read to him, but if caught reading it he would be severely lashed. As late as July, 1847, Martha Christian, a Virginia slave-mistress, was given two years of imprisonment for teaching her slave to read. The indictment read, "For not having the fear of God upon her eyes, but moved by the devil, wickedly, maliciously, and feloniously did teach a black woman, Rebecca, alias Black Beck, to read the Bible, to great displeasure of Almighty God."

Even today we read and hear sermons to the effect that the Negro is subhuman. One denomination I am told professes to believe that the Negro is without a soul. Such degrading and dehumanizing of the Negro is criminal and satanic. Such evil brainwashing perverts the thinking of Negroes and affects their daily lives and outlook on life. Many become discouraged. Others experience an inner psychological struggle which they are unable to overcome. Others resign themselves to the fact that they can never be anything more than stepchildren of God and second-class citizens of America. This explains why many Negroes reject the Christian church, the Bible, and

134

Jesus Christ, turning instead to false cults and religions. They are earnestly seeking an answer to their racial identity and purpose for being in the world. There is an alarming increase in the number of suicides among Negroes. Why? For the simple reason that if God is prejudiced against them because of their race, what hope do they have? And if they become frustrated and despondent in the civil-rights fight for freedom, what incentive do they have for living?

In a recent newspaper was the report of a Negro woman who reached this place of hopelessness in life. Locking herself in her home, she put the song "We Shall Overcome!" on the record player, read her Bible, prayed, and then shot herself. Her suicide note stated that she was "tired of fighting not only whites for the cause of civil rights, but Negroes who seem ungrateful."

Perhaps the prime reason why most white Christians hold tenaciously to racist views is their fear of interracial marriage. This subject almost always crops up in my own discussions. The question, "Would you want your daughter to marry a Negro?" haunts them.

But does the Negro really seek integration for the purpose of intermarriage with the whites? Of course not! The great majority of Negroes are utterly disinterested in interracial marriages. In the North where Negroes and whites have been more closely associated than in the South, only a small number of interracial marriages have occurred.

It would be foolish, however, to deny that interracial marriages do at times occur. In such cases it is a personal matter between two persons, one which either can decide against if he chooses. Too often the subject of interracial marriage has merely been an excuse for race prejudice.

In talking with white Christians I have discovered that they are extremely sensitive about this matter. A Negro student at one of our outstanding Bible schools informed me that at the opening of the school year the white girls were warned by the dean that they must not date Negroes or any other foreigners.

This step was taken as a precaution against courtships which could lead to interracial marriages. Similar action has been taken in other Christian schools.

A white minister who served as pastor of a Negro church resigned when his daughters reached teen-age, lest they become involved with some of the Negro young men in the church.

Two Negro minister friends and I were panelists at a Christian literature conference sponsored by one of the leading Christian magazines. The editors and writers fired questions at us on the race problem as related to the Christian church. At the close of the session four men approached me and asked: "Howard, don't you agree that an interracial marriage is both contrary to Scripture and illegal?"

"No, I do not," I replied.

"Why?"

"Well," I said, "if two people fulfill all the requirements of the law and are married, their marriage is not illegal. And the only way that a marriage would be contrary to Scripture is for a Christian to marry an unconverted person and thereby move outside of the will of God. As far as interracial marriage is concerned, I find nothing in the Bible to condemn it. Rather, I find where God smote Miriam with leprosy because she murmured against Moses when he married an Ethiopian woman."

Another of the men said: "Howard, you have three daughters. Now just for the sake of argument, suppose one of your daughters fell in love with a young white man, and the two decided that they wanted to get married. What would your reaction be?"

My reply was that I would oppose such a marriage because it would be unwise in view of the present social structure in this country. I would explain to my daughter that while it might be lawful for her to marry a young white man, it would not be expedient. Such marriage would present additional problems, especially in the rearing of children. She would undoubtedly experience ostracism by the whites, as would her husband by Negroes. I would try to make her understand that an interracial marriage in the present American society is one which would require many personal adjustments and sacrifices for any couple, and that the road ahead would certainly be a rocky one.

I would explain my viewpoint to the young man. But if, after all my counsel and advice, this young couple felt that they were in the will of God in this marriage and were willing to face the many problems and difficulties with faith in Christ, what could I say? I would have to accept their decision, grant my permission, and pray that God's richest blessing might be upon them. Then both my wife and I would do all in our power to help them make a success of their marriage. "Would you gentlemen agree with my position?" I concluded.

They agreed that I could be expected to take no other course of action.

Let us look at the race problem in light of the Bible. What does the Word of God have to say about it? The practice of segregation and discrimination against a person because of color or race is certainly not sustained by the Scriptures. Racism in any form, whether in the church or nation, is a sin in the sight of God. Why? Because God is love, and anything that is contrary to this love is unlike God, and therefore is sin.

The Epistle of First John deals with race relations in the Christian perspective, and here we read: "He that saith he is in the light, and hateth his brother, is in darkness even until now. He that loveth his brother abideth in the light, and there is none occasion of stumbling in him. But he that hateth his brother is in darkness, and walketh in darkness, and knoweth not whither he goeth, because that darkness hath blinded his eyes. . . . For this is the message that ye heard from the beginning, that we should love one another. Not as Cain, who was of that wicked one, and slew his brother. And wherefore slew he him? Because his own works were evil, and his brother's righteous. . . . We know that we have passed from death unto life, because we love the brethren. He that loveth not his brother abideth in death. Whosoever hateth his brother is a murderer: and ye know that no murderer hath eternal life abiding in him. . . . But whoso hath this world's good, and seeth his brother have need, and shutteth up his bowels of compassion from him, how dwelleth the love of God in him?" (I JOHN 2:9-11; 3:11-12,14,15,17).

Or consider the admonition of James: "If ye fulfill the royal law according to the scripture, Thou shalt love thy neighbour as thyself, ye do well: But if ye have respect to persons, ye commit sin, and are convinced of the law as transgressors. For whosoever shall keep the whole law, and yet offend in one point, he is guilty of all" (JAMES 2:8-10).

In the light of such teaching, does it not behoove white Christians to stop making excuses for their prejudices and un-Christian attitudes toward the Negro? The fact must be faced that racism is just as much a sin as murder, stealing, lying, cheating, and immorality. God will assuredly judge those who break the royal commandment, "Thou shalt love thy neighbour as thyself."

Too long have racist ideas and feelings been harbored within the framework of Christianity. The monster must be dragged into the open and destroyed. White ministers must preach against this ugly sin which destroys the witness of the church and makes it a laughingstock before the world. The church must cease to practice racial segregation and discrimination because they are morally wrong. They deprive the Negro of his right to have and to be.

Dr. Benjamin J. Mays says: "Segregation on the basis of color or race is a wicked thing because it penalizes a person for being what God has made him and for conditions over which he has no control. If one were segregated because of ignorance, he could learn and change the situation. If one were segregated because of poverty, he could work and improve the economic status. If he were segregated because of uncleanliness,

138

he could bathe and become acceptable. But if one is segregated and stigmatized because of his race, he is penalized for something which he cannot change. And to do this is tantamount to saying to God, 'You made a mistake when you made people of different races and colors.'"

In light of the present conflict many people are asking, "Is there any real hope for a solution of the race problem before us?" Yes, there is a solution. First, we must insist on the establishment of better laws and the enforcement of those laws throughout the land, but we must go further than that. Since the race problem is basically a moral and spiritual one, we must take a spiritual approach. We shall get at the heart of the race problem by getting at the hearts of both Negro and whites, and only Jesus Christ can do that. Christ is the final answer.

Both white and Negro Christians often agree that Christ fundamentally is the answer to the race problem, but with many this has become a cliché, a religious shibboleth they use to ease their consciences. "Christ is the answer to the race problem," they say, yet continue merrily down the road of prejudice and bigotry. We must allow Christ to solve this problem in our own hearts before we can expect to see a change in the church and community. The very fact that such a problem exists in the church proves that something is radically wrong with us as Christians. Have we truly been converted? When people of different races come to the cross and receive Christ as Saviour, experiencing the saving grace and love of God in their lives, they become brothers in the Lord and love one another with a pure heart fervently. In their relationship as believers, racial differences are lost in the spiritual union they find in Christ. Then why is there so little evidence of such spiritual union among Negro and white Christians? Is it because we are not really born again, or are mere "babes in Christ," immature children of God?

The Apostle Paul tells us how God took the Gentiles and Jews and blended them together into one new man, one body through Christ and His Gospel. The enmity which existed between the Jews and Gentiles was done away by the work of Christ on the cross, and peace prevailed. To both the redeemed Jews and Gentiles, Paul could say: "For through him [Christ] we both have access by one Spirit unto the Father. Now therefore ye are no more strangers and foreigners, but fellowcitizens with the saints, and of the household of God" (EPHESIANS 2:18,19).

To the Colossians the apostle also stressed this spiritual unity when he declared: "Where there is neither Greek nor Jew, circumcision nor uncircumcision, Barbarian, Scythian, bond nor free: but Christ is all, and in all" (COLOSSIANS 3:11).

Since God performed this miracle of bringing the Jew and Gentile into fellowship in His Son, Jesus Christ, by removing their sins and the racial prejudice, animosity, and hatred between them, why are we so slow to believe that this same God is able to blend Negro and white Christians into a similar fellowship in our time? If the Bible tells us that there is no difference in Christ, then why do we make such a differentiation between races in the church? The fact that we do differentiate proves that we have lost the concept of the "true church," the body of Christ. We must rediscover the meaning of the church and recognize the position that all born-again believers hold in that church. The church must demonstrate the truth that as Christians we are one in Christ, regardless of race and nationality, and that all racial barriers lie shattered at the foot of His cross.

It is significant that during the Billy Graham crusades in Birmingham, Alabama, in 1963 and in Montgomery in 1965, there was such a demonstration. Under the preaching of the cross of Christ, Negroes and whites met together in integrated meetings which made history. The message of the Gospel brought conviction of sin to the hearts of the people, and at the evangelist's invitation hundreds came to receive Christ as their Saviour. For the first time people representing both races found Christ to be the answer to all problems, including race prejudice and hatred. What God accomplished in those crusades in saving souls and breaking down the wall of bigotry, He can do in any local church. But how many of our ministers and churches would be happy about it?

As I see the race problem from the Christian standpoint, I am convinced that only Christ can give us the capacity to love all men, even our enemies. Jesus, being a Jew, suffered the sting of race prejudice at the hands of the Samaritans. In the Gospel of Luke we read the following account: "And it came to pass, when the time was come that he should be received up, he stedfastly set his face to go to Jerusalem, And sent messengers before his face: and they went, and entered into a village of the Samaritans, to make ready for him. And they did not receive him, because his face was as though he would go to Jerusalem. And when his disciples James and John saw this, they said, Lord, wilt thou that we command fire to come down from heaven, and consume them, even as Elias did? But he turned, and rebuked them, and said, Ye know not what manner of spirit ye are of. For the Son of man is not come to destroy men's lives, but to save them. And they went to another village" (LUKE 9:51-56).

Here we have two reactions set forth in a humiliating experience our Lord encountered with the Samaritans. First there is the reaction toward violence and revenge reflected by James and John. Then there is the reaction of love revealed by Jesus. In the racial conflict of our day there is the need for a reaction of love on the part of all Christians. This love cannot be manufactured; it must be ". . . shed abroad in our hearts by the Holy Ghost . . ." (ROMANS 5:5). This love will enable us even to love those who hate us.

During my early Christian experience I had to learn this lesson. Once when my father and I were driving home from a visit to a nearby city we experienced car trouble. We pulled over to the side of the road just as it was beginning to get dark, and, with headlights turned on, we went to work. Then we heard loud noises from a group of men emerging from a bar. They were drunk, and, as they staggered toward us, one of them called out: "Hey, look at those niggers over there fooling with that car. I bet they stole it. Come on, let's get them."

Two of the men ran over, grabbed me, and knocked me to the ground. They began to kick and swing their fists at me, but I was able to protect myself because they were so drunk. My father came from behind the car and to my aid, but as he did so a policeman approached and bellowed: "Stand back; don't you interfere; I have my hand on my gun."

My father stepped back, while the two men continued to attack me. Another man laughed and hurled abusive remarks at both of us. Finally, the policeman ordered the men to cease their attack. Turning to my father, he said: "I want you to get this car started and get out of here, and I mean business."

As we drove away my father said: "Son, I am glad you are not hurt. I trust that I will never see those men again, for if I do there will be trouble."

Naturally I was grateful that I had not been seriously hurt or perhaps killed by those racists whose lawlessness against us as Negroes had been permitted and encouraged by the policeman. But neither the brutality of the men nor the callousness of the officer of the law caused me to hate them. As a Christian I knew I dare not hate my enemies.

America continues to spawn hate groups who spread their evil influence everywhere. The "mystery of iniquity" is at work in their minds and hearts. Ku Klux Klansmen desecrate the Christian's cross by burning it as a symbol of their hatred for Negroes and other minority groups. And there are the sinister operations of such groups as the White Citizens Council, the Minutemen, and the American Nazi Party.

Nor is the Negro race blameless, considering the activities of the Black Muslims, the Five Percenters, and others who sow their seeds of antiwhite propaganda in the minds of Negroes. Such racists—black and white—are setting the stage in America for a bloody race war. Even in the church at times one senses a spirit of hate, bitterness, and revenge. Many trace this to hate groups which have infiltrated the church.

Recently I was told of a white minister who keeps a loaded gun in the pulpit, and boasts: "I am going to shoot the first nigger that walks through that door."

A Negro minister said: "I believe that Malcolm X's policy of violence was right. If we must use violence to get our rights, I am for it."

A white minister who was driven from his pulpit over this issue observed: "I am a pessimist. I believe that a bloodbath will eventually result from the race issue."

Violence and bloodshed are not the answer to the race problem Jesus Christ warned: ". . . all they that take the sword shall perish with the sword" (MATTHEW 26:52).

President Johnson, protesting the violence and riots in Los Angeles, said: "A rioter with a Molotov cocktail in his hands is not fighting for civil rights anymore than a Klansman with a sheet on his back and a mask on his face. They are both more or less what the law declares them: Lawbreakers, destroyers of constitutional rights and liberties, and would ultimately destroy a free America. And they must be exposed and dealt with."

It is my strong conviction that without Jesus Christ we shall never solve the race problem. The solution is not hate but love, a love which flows from the heart of God into our own. It is the kind of love Jesus exhibited on the cross when He looked down upon His enemies and prayed: "Father, forgive them, for they know not what they do."

Only a baptism in the love and compassion of Christ can smother the hot flames of racial prejudice, bitterness, and hatred in the hearts of men. Unless a moral and spiritual awakening comes soon, America may find herself involved in another civil war, in which the blood of both races will stain the streets of our towns and cities.

But such a catastrophe can be avoided if there is a spiritual revival in our churches. Christians are praying, pleading, and weeping before God for revival, and God knows that the church needs a fresh breath of spiritual life and power from heaven. But it is exceedingly doubtful that God is going to effect such a revival until the church comes to grips with the sin of racism and repents and forsakes it. We have no reason to expect revival until both Negro and white Christians meet Christ anew, overcome their prejudice and bitterness, and allow God to cleanse their hearts.

In this crucial hour we can afford no longer to compromise. Such will prove a disaster for the church and the nation. Gordon W. Allport, Harvard University's eminent social psychologist, warns us: "The day of reckoning has come for the Christian Church. The world is now too crowded, too perilous and too rapidly changing to permit further temporizing with bigotry and discrimination. . . . The task is difficult, the challenge is immediate."

The Christian church therefore must become the light of the world and the salt of the earth in every area of life. Only as Christians who are cleansed of attitudes of segregation and discrimination and who are baptized with the love of God and love for one another can we stem the rising tide of violence, hatred, and bloodshed now confronting us. We must quit evading the issue and making excuses. We must stop being overcome with race prejudice and bitterness. As Negro and white Christians let us allow Christ to settle the problem once and for all. Let us not be satisfied until we have overcome.

LIFT EVERY VOICE AND SING
(National Negro Anthem)
JAMES WELDON JOHNSON

Lift every voice and sing
Till earth and heaven ring,
Ring with the harmonies of liberty;
Let our rejoicing rise
High as the listening skies,
Let it resound loud as the rolling sea.
Sing a song full of the faith that the dark past has taught us,
Sing a song full of the hope that the present has brought us,
Facing the rising sun of our new day begun
Let us march on till victory is won.

Stony the road we trod,
Bitter the chastening rod,
Felt in the days when hope unborn had died;
Yet with a steady beat,
Have not our weary feet
Come to the place for which our fathers sighed?
We have come over a way that with tears has been watered,
We have come, treading our path through the blood of the
    slaughtered,
Out from the gloomy past,
Till now we stand at last
Where the white gleam of our bright star is cast.

God of our weary years,
God of our silent tears,
Thou who has brought us thus far on the way;
Thou who has by Thy might
Led us into the light,
Keep us forever in the path, we pray.
Lest our feet stray from the places, our God, where we met
    Thee,
Lest, hearts drunk with the wine of the world, we forget Thee;
Shadowed beneath Thy hand,
May we forever stand.
True to our God,
True to our native land.